Kieran Hurley
Plays 1

Kieran Hurley is a playwright from Edinburgh, Scotland. He started out making shows at the Arches in Glasgow, a now-defunct performance art venue and nightclub underneath the city's Central Station where he also worked in the cloakroom. Since then he has worked closely with the Traverse Theatre, the National Theatre of Scotland and others, with his plays being performed in multiple translations across the world. His debut screenplay *Beats* was co-written with director Brian Welsh and adapted from his breakout play of the same name. With his partner and frequent collaborator Julia Taudevin he is co-Artistic Director of the theatre company Disaster Plan. They live in Glasgow, with their two children.

Kieran Hurley
Plays 1

Hitch
Beats
Heads Up
Mouthpiece
The Enemy

With an introduction by
JOYCE McMILLAN

methuen | drama

LONDON · NEW YORK · OXFORD · NEW DELHI · SYDNEY

METHUEN DRAMA
Bloomsbury Publishing Plc
50 Bedford Square, London, WC1B 3DP, UK
1385 Broadway, New York, NY 10018, USA
29 Earlsfort Terrace, Dublin 2, Ireland

BLOOMSBURY, METHUEN DRAMA and the Methuen Drama logo are
trademarks of Bloomsbury Publishing Plc

This collection first published in Great Britain 2023

Hitch first published in this collection by Methuen Drama 2023
Copyright © Kieran Hurley, 2023

Beats first published by Oberon Books in 2013
Copyright © Kieran Hurley, 2013

Heads Up first published by Oberon Books in 2017
Copyright © Kieran Hurley, 2017

Mouthpiece first published by Oberon Books in 2018
Copyright © Kieran Hurley, 2018

The Enemy first published by Methuen Drama in 2021
Copyright © Kieran Hurley, 2021

A catalogue record for this book is available from the British Library.

A catalog record for this book is available from the Library of Congress.

ISBN: PB: 978-1-3503-3478-6
ePDF: 978-1-3503-3479-3
eBook: 978-1-3503-3480-9

Series: Contemporary Dramatists

Typeset by RefineCatch Limited, Bungay, Suffolk
Printed and bound in Great Britain

To find out more about our authors and books visit www.bloomsbury.com
and sign up for our newsletters.

For Kathleen

Contents

Introduction

When I first heard Kieran Hurley's name, in July 2009, it was attached to an installation that – as part of a festival of new work – had been placed in a small vaulted cellar, somewhere in the dark depths of the Arches in Glasgow. Someone, it seemed, had gone to Italy, to take part in the protests and demonstrations surrounding that year's G8 summit of world leaders; and as part of the installation, he would be sending back messages that would somehow make their way into the cellar, and appear on a map fixed to the wall.

I saw no messages arriving; bad timing, no doubt. But I learned that the person who had made that journey was Kieran Hurley, one of a group of young Glasgow University theatre graduates then involved in making experimental work at the Arches; and when I returned in the autumn to see his more fully-fledged show *Hitch*, based on his Italian experience, I expected something equally visual and non-text-based, in keeping with the mood of a venue – part night club and music venue, part gallery, part theatre – where the very idea of theatre was being challenged and reinvented week after week, under the artistic directorship first of Andy Arnold, and then of Jackie Wylie, now artistic director of the National Theatre of Scotland.

What Kieran Hurley delivered that night, though, was more like an enthralling and beautifully-written piece of storytelling, with powerful musical accompaniment, about his journey and its many meanings, both political and personal. The sheer quality and rhythmic power of the text stood out, among so much work in which text was secondary; although Hurley had until that point been almost entirely a collaborative theatre-maker and performer – acting in shows, and co-directing with a collective of other young theatre-makers. While collaborative relationships forged around this time would continue through his later work – not least of all with fellow playwright Gary McNair and Hurley's future wife, the writer and actor Julia Taudevin – *Hitch* set him on the path towards something more like a career in play-writing.

In 2011, he was joint winner of the Arches Platform 18 award, aimed at giving young directors a budget to create the show of their choice; and this time, in collaboration with DJ Johnny Whoop and and VJ Jamie Wardrop, Hurley produced *Beats*, another spellbinding tale told as a monologue, with a beautiful narrative arc, about a teenage boy caught in that 1990s moment when the Criminal Justice and Public Order Act (1996) outlawed any public gathering characterized by 'the emission of a succession of repetitive beats'.

Premiered at the Arches in the spring of 2012, and then transferred to the Traverse during that year's Edinburgh Fringe, *Beats* opened a whole range of doors for Hurley, not only to formal new play commissions from the Traverse and other theatres, but also to the world of screen-writing. After its Fringe appearance, there was immediate substantial interest in transforming *Beats* into a film; and the film version, directed by Brian Welsh, was finally released in 2019, to overwhelmingly positive reviews.

In the past decade, Kieran Hurley's career as a playwright and theatre-maker has evolved at speed, to the point where he is now one of the most successful and sought-after Scottish stage and screen writers of his generation. Yet even in those early works, *Hitch* and *Beats* – which open this new Methuen collection of his plays – the main hallmarks of his work were present and well-marked: intense political awareness combined with deep human engagement and empathy, an endless willingness to experiment with form and to be an active performer and theatre-maker as well as a writer, and a gift for storytelling that often combines a taut and beautiful narrative structure with a powerful strand of poetry.

Kieran Hurley was born in Edinburgh in 1986, one of triplets – all boys – born to parents who already had a son and a daughter. His father, Fintan, is Irish; and Hurley traces some of his powerful sense of what theatre could be back to the experience, when he was thirteen or fourteen, of being taken by his father to see Mark O'Rowe's *Howie The Rookie* at the Assembly Rooms, and marvelling at the theatrical intensity that two entwined monologues could achieve. At Holy Rood High School in Edinburgh, Hurley was also taught by two legendary drama teachers, Frances Paterson and Pat Crichton, who helped inspire many potential actors, writers and directors into theatre careers; and of course, along with the rest of his generation, he was growing up in a Scotland changed forever by the political events of the Thatcher years, a country which – when Hurley was thirteen –

regained its parliament, just a couple of miles from Hurley's school, after a gap of almost 300 years.

All of these factors no doubt contributed to Hurley's formation as a writer; and after the initial success of *Beats*, he plunged straight into the politics of the day, working with Julia Taudevin to co-write *Chalk Farm*, a furiously vivid play about the London riots of 2011, seen at the Play, Pie And Pint lunchtime theatre in Glasgow in 2012. That year, for the National Theatre of Scotland, he also wrote *Rantin'*, premiered in 2013, an early piece of 'gig theatre' which combined music played and sung by a band with short narrative glimpses of contemporary Scottish lives.

At this stage, Hurley was already working – both alone and collaboratively – on several more formal play commissions; and in 2015, one of those emerged as a village hall touring production for Perth Theatre, *A Six Inch Layer of Topsoil and the Fact that It Rains*, which used not only music and song, but also documentary techniques often used to give a voice to socially excluded groups, to describe the lives of Perthshire farmers in the period just before the Brexit vote. Hurley was also working with fellow writer Gary McNair on the script that would eventually become their 2018 Edinburgh Fringe hit *Square Go*, an intensely physical choreographed play about male violence and toxic masculinity from the playground into adult life.

At this stage, though, he also felt a powerful need to return to the simplicity and freedom of monologue performance of his own work, with which his career had begun; and at the Edinburgh Fringe of 2016, in a small room at Summerhall, he premiered *Heads Up*, a superb, beautifully-paced apocalyptic poem which he performed from his own sound and effects desk, like a DJ playing out a set that includes his own visionary words. Full of a profound sense of a western urban civilization hurtling towards destruction, *Heads Up* conjured a cityscape both immensely familiar and completely strange, poised on the brink of catastrophe; and it was a huge Fringe hit, transferring to London early in 2017.

Hurley also still had a commission from the Traverse Theatre to fulfil, working with the theatre's artistic director from 2012 until 2018, Orla O'Loughlin; and at Christmas 2018, soon after the Fringe success of *Square Go*, the Traverse premiered *Mouthpiece*, Hurley's beautiful, timely and prescient two-handed drama about class and creativity in the UK today. Set in the famously divided city of Edinburgh – and sometimes even in the Traverse auditorium itself – the play revolves around an encounter between Libby, a forty-something playwright who has returned to Edinburgh after failing to make it in London, and Declan, a fiery young working-class man whom she meets one evening on Salisbury Crags; and it deals both savagely and eloquently with the expropriation of working-class experience, and working-class voices, by middle-class writers trying to add an edge to their work, and middle-class audiences in search of thrills and 'authenticity'. The play transferred to Soho Theatre in London early in 2019, and returned to the Traverse during the Edinburgh Festival of 2019, winning international acclaim.

When the Covid pandemic hit in the spring of 2020, Hurley's next project – a major twenty-first century adaptation of Ibsen's *An Enemy of the People* for the National Theatre of Scotland, due to open a nationwide tour in April 2020 – was one of the first to be postponed, with no immediate prospect of reappearing; but it was also, in Finn den Hertog's memorable production, one of the first to re-emerge after Scottish theatre began to reopen, and in October 2021, *The Enemy* was premiered at Dundee Rep to huge acclaim, before touring on to Edinburgh, Inverness and Perth.

It was all too short a run, though, for a brilliant new version of Ibsen's drama, with such a thorough and clear-sighted grasp of the play's essential conflicts between money, power and inconvenient scientific truth – all filtered through the flawed amplifier of the media – that it seems both completely faithful to Ibsen's original 1882 text, and as if it might have been written yesterday, for the age of pandemics, climate crisis and savagely judgemental social media; and it richly deserves a wider audience.

Today, Kieran Hurley lives in Glasgow with Julia Taudevin and their two young children. Together, they have launched a company called Disaster Plan, which is currently touring a revival of Taudevin's beautiful 2021 show *Move*, performed on beaches across Scotland, about the movement of people down the ages; the next Disaster Plan show, Hurley says, will be based on a script of his.

Otherwise, though, he says that he has never had a plan for his career in theatre, and has none now; nor does he see his work undergoing any conventional evolution from early experiments with solo and collective theatre-making, to more conventional play-writing for large casts and many characters. Instead, he sees all the elements of his work – the formal experiments, the storytelling, the solo performance, the collaborations, the screen writing, the more conventional playwriting – as intertwined strands of the same creative process, which come to the surface depending on the subject in hand. 'Yesterday,' he says, 'I had an idea for a play with four or five characters, which is just going to have to be written that way. But I've also got an idea for a new monologue which is to some extent by and about me, which I'll have to write and perform myself. That's how it's always been, for me, and that's how I like it; always shifting from one approach to another, depending on what the story demands – and always willing to try something completely new, if that's what it takes.'

Joyce McMillan
Edinburgh
July 2022

Hitch

Kieran Hurley

Hitch was first premiered at Arches Live festival at the Arches, Glasgow in September 2009. It was later presented at Forest Fringe at the Forest Café in Edinburgh in August 2010 before touring across the UK and internationally. The team was as follows:

Writer: Kieran Hurley
Co-directors: Kieran Hurley, Julia Taudevin, Dick Bonham, Jamie Fletcher
Music: Ben Hillman and Gav Prentice
Video: Julia Taudevin
Lights: Briony Berning

A note on the original production

Hitch is an autobiographical story, originally performed by myself alongside two musicians, Ben Hillman and Gav Prentice of Over The Wall, with their music soundtracking the piece throughout. The stage was empty apart from a microphone on a mic stand, which was used only occasionally. There was a screen at the back of the space which projected images, video, and text variously throughout. The space should always feel informal, the audience aware of each other.

Scene One

I'd like to start by saying thank you. To

Harry, who had to get up really early to help me again

Gem, who told me to ask the boss

Stanley, who is four years old (well, he's about six now actually)

Pete, who used to have a green Mohawk and build a nuclear weapons programme

Wendy, who was going to a wedding

Robin, who said I reminded him of his youth

Jane, who used to work in prisons

Fred, who I lived with before

Jo, who wondered why it hadn't taken longer, and who called me 'love'

Thank you also to boy Joe, Clare, and Rhi, who played Singstar, Pro Ev, and Ring of Fire

Thank you to Igor who welcomed me, a stranger, with open arms

To Bruno, who loves plants, and cats, and hates the heat

Gabriel, who is searching for an original sound

And Ilija, who speaks seven languages and eats cheese and frozen meat

Michel, who is well-measured

Sami, who is emphatic

Franck, who is patient

Giulia, who is an angel who I have never met

Claudio, who was my Bologna brother, who would not share a bed

Noemi, who figured everything out in the end

Irma, who nursed me and fed me in the Sanctuary

and Gwen, who brought me crashing back to familiar ground in style

and I'd like to thank you

and you

and this guy here

Thanks all of you, for coming.

Scene Two

His red hard hat catches the sun.
It flickers in my eyes.
He turns to me and says
Yes.
And you are our neighbour now.

We've come as far as we can go. The helicopters overhead are lower now. Their rhythmic mechanical pulsing shakes the air. We breathe and move together. We are pushed back, we sway. I feel a strangers hand grip my shoulder and keep me up. We raise our hands in peace. We raise our voices in song. And slowly, slowly . . .

He screams.

Scene Three

It's June 2009, and Michael Jackson has just died.

Barack Obama has been sworn into office and has announced he will send more troops to Afghanistan.

Australia has just suffered its worst bush fires in recorded history and we've all seen the pictures on the news of billowing smoke and swathes of land in flames.

L'Aquila, in Italy, a town near Rome, has just been destroyed by an earthquake, prompting Silvio Berlusconi to relocate the G8 meeting of leaders of that year to the town of L'Aquila in a hollow PR stunt.

Gordon Brown is our Prime Minister and it looks more and more likely that we'll soon have a Tory government for the first time since I was eleven, though any sense of how it could be all that much worse feels, at the moment, to me, like a kind of distant, imagined abstraction.

Newcastle United have just been relegated and everyone is getting all het up about something called swine flu. It's like bird flu apparently, but worse.

And there's me, in my old room in the top floor of that big shared flat on Woodlands Road, stuffing my rucksack to the involuntary soundtrack of Billie Jean and Smooth Criminal blaring from open windows and passing cars from the street below. And I'm wondering how I'm going to get there. And I'm racking my brains to try to remember why on earth I decided to do this in the first place.

Well.

It started with a fear. A frustration. A confusion. Knowing full well that the world was moving in a direction and shifting in a way that was beyond my control and beyond the control of anyone I could trust.

It started with not knowing what my future was. Not in the job sense, or life plan sense. But something bigger.

It started with a loneliness, a worry, a sadness looking out over the lights of cars, the rows of red and white at Charing Cross motorway at night. Thinking of how I was once told that we spend more time in our lives at traffic lights than we do kissing. Listening to the motorway sounding like the sea and knowing that I had to get the hell out of here.

It started, aged fifteen the last time the G8 went to Italy and I read about how that boy died. That boy Carlo Giuliani. And I read about how the police shot him in the head. And I wondered how it could happen. He wasn't much older than me. And I obsessed about it for weeks.

Maybe it started in 2005, when they came here to Scotland. And I thought again about Carlo. And I stayed at home, and never forgave myself.

It started when I heard they were going to be in Italy again. It started with no other summer plans. With no money. No travel ticket and no willingness to get on a plane.

It really started with a pint in a Glasgow pub. A fantastical thought, an idea, a challenge, a muttered question: why don't you just go?

So I did.

On the 8 July 2009, the leaders of the eight most powerful countries in the world met in the small earthquake stricken town of L'Aquila in Italy, to make plans for the future of our society and our planet.

On the morning of Saturday the 27 June, I left my flat in Glasgow, and stuck out my thumb, to be there too.

Scene Four

Transition.

Video of packing in bedroom, then of hitching at Hamilton.

Music.

Scene Five

Hamilton Service Station.

8.27am, Saturday 27 June 2009.

It is grey.
It is brown.
It is green.
With a hint of straw.

Standing.

Standing.

It's a tiring business, this, standing.

I'm standing by the side of the slip road at the services exit, over 1,500 miles from L'Aquila. I've been dropped here by good my friend Harry who has kindly agreed to give me a lift out of town, but now, I stand here, alone.

I have with me a rucksack, and a cardboard sign saying 'SOUTH'.

I have politely added the word 'please' for those drivers who care to read the small print.

It is not helping.

I stand here, alone, thumb-out, making my best hopeful-yet-friendly face.

It doesn't work.

A change of tact is needed. I pack away the sign, give my thumb a rest and make my way over to the Wild Bean Café – you know the one. If nobody will stop and ask me where I'm going then I'll just have to stop them and ask them where they are going.

And it works. After an hour or so of
Excuse me, I'm sorry to bother you, you wouldn't be driving south to England, would you?
I have my first lift.
And I'm off.

Scene Six

A bust card.

A bust card is an information leaflet circulated at demonstrations by the organisers.

It offers information on what to do should you get into trouble with the authorities, as well as advice on how to organise effectively in order to avoid this. Usually, it will also display an emergency legal support number you can call if you are in need.

As you will see, the bust card becomes important to this story on a bus somewhere in the countryside of Lazio, when the girl sitting next to me hands me this one, causing me to panic.

Scene Seven

The people who give me my first lift are a couple Gem and Pete, and their four-year-old son, Stanley.

I'd approached Gem at first but she simply gestured over her shoulder, telling me I should ask the boss. The boss was Pete. A large, muscular man with a shaved head, and a formidable meaty face pierced by two keen blue eyes.
He was on the phone.
It seemed important.
I decided I'd rather not bother him.
But ten minutes later, Pete approached me and asked,

Where you off to, son?

London, eventually. You?

Stoke-on-Trent. Not through choice. Get in, I'll take you as far as Knutsford. Hitch-hikers' paradise there.

I throw my bag over my shoulder and nearly fall over with gratitude as I make my way towards the car.

They are going to Stoke-on-Trent, it turns out, to visit Gem's parents. Gem sits in the back with Stanley, and Pete does all the talking. He slags off the in-laws, he slags off Stoke-on-Trent, he slags off, amongst other things, the nation of Australia, and the sport of tennis. Turns out Pete's first job was working on the

Liverpool docks aged sixteen building vanguard vessels for the Trident nuclear weapons programme. He didn't know what it was when he signed up for it.

He sacked it off in the end. Said it was shit.

A punk rocker in his time, he wasn't shy of a riot or two, and he still talks proudly of the green Mohawk he sported in his youth.

This is me.
In the passenger seat.
I'm wearing a bright orange t-shirt and dark blue jeans.
I'm twenty-three years old.
I feel nervous.
But also relieved and excited.
Notice the way I spend the first hour of journey fiddling with my finger nails and readjusting my feet.

He holds this position, before moving to become **Pete**.

I tell you one thing though, one thing that really gets my goat, is the eco-toffs. It's a sort of green fascism really with the eco-toffs. Look at what they're saying about, say, Ethiopia – ooh, ooh, oh no look at you planning to mine for coal, shock horror. I mean coal's fine when it allows us all to get rich enough off to ponce around for a bit at uni, but you, little nation of African people that want to develop, please, think of the planet first! Condescening cunts.

I change the subject. I say

When I get to Italy, I'm planning on going to the G8 demonstrations

Bloody do it son. Watch out for them Italian riot cops though they're not a nice bunch. Killed that young lad last time, didn't they, what was his name, Carlo, Carlo Giuliani. That's him. Shot him, square in the head. Wouldn't want to see that happen to you would we?

For a while we bond over my intention of being at the G8 protests, Pete attempts some advice on finding anarchist squats in Rome and reminisces on his own protest days of old. Eventually, he says

You know it won't do nowt though don't ya? All these big protests an' that, like G20 and that, it's all well and good but what is it really just a big walk from A down to B, and then home again for tea. It doesn't make any difference. Fuck all changes anyway, no matter what you do. What do you think you'll actually change by being there eh?

We sit in silence for a while, for this first time since I got into the car.

Eventually Gem, Pete, and Stanley leave me at Knutsford services. Hitch-hikers' paradise according to the man himself. As I get out of the car, Pete's parting words to me are

Get yourself to that G20 or whatever. Chuck a brick in a cop's face from me.

I smile in gratitude, shake his hand in comradeship, and don't quite muster up the courage to tell him that was never really part of my original plan.

Scene Eight

Recorded voice:

london four forty seven am sunday the twenty eighth of june two thousand and nine

head pressed to pillow and belly and mind full of beer and heart warmth

comfort here

i lie with my back pressed to the mattress becomes ground

becomes grass

sound of cars birds

clouds move above me and i realise that the earth

is moving and i lie pressed against it

insects buzz and grass stretches out

growing around my ears

i roll over slide onto my side slide onto front and crawl onto a pavement cold hard

teeth pressed on concrete

naked skin on grit and stone

and shard of light pierce through the gaps

slowly

i lift up the paving stones

one by

one

and find bright light

fresh air

of the beach beneath them

Scene Nine

[This is the French I speak.].

Je'mappelle Kieran

[My name is Kieran.]

Bonjour.

[Hello.]

Merci.

[Thank you.]

Pardon. Je ne parle pas Francais.

[Sorry. I don't speak French.]

[This is the Italian I speak.]

Mi chiamo Kieran.

[My name is Kieran.]

Buongiorno.

[Hello.]

Grazie

[Thank you.]

Ciao.

[Hello/goodbye (informal).]

Sono l'artista autostopista.

[I am a hitch-hiking artist.]

Scene Ten

Transition.

Video. Distance from Glasgow to Paris.

Music.

Scene Eleven

Outside Gare du Nord, Paris, France.

6.30pm.

Monday 29 June.

It is light blue.
It is muted white.
It is deep red.
It is concrete grey.
People.
Smoke.

I've just arrived in Paris and it is hot. Very hot. Later tonight, I'll find out that this week has been exceptionally and extraordinarily hot for Parisian standards, but for now I'm content to believe that this is just what the weather is like here.

I'm suddenly aware of being quite far from home.

Outside the station, I dump by my bag on the ground, sit on it, and a roll myself a cigarette.
As I do this, I somehow make eye contact with a man across the street. His gaze locks on mine, and slowly, he begins to walk towards me.

Look at him, coming closer. He has a grey beard, leathery sun-darkened skin and a big weather-beaten old jacket that he simply must be boiling in. Most strikingly he wears a big bright yellow hat, with a wide brim like a cartoon Stetson. His skin and clothes are dirty. I presume he is homeless, but I can't tell of course. As he comes closer, I see that his eyes are a thick black-brown, like a deep polluted river.

He stands next to me now. He leans down beside me, beckons with his left hand, and in a gentle voice, he asks me if he can have a cigarette.

He asks in English. Straight off. How did he know? Is it that obvious to everyone here that I'm an outsider or is this man just amazingly perceptive? Maybe it was just a good guess. I shuffle around trying to find my cigarette papers. They're not in the tobacco packet, not in my jean pockets, they're nowhere. I look at him. And he tells me

You are nervous.

I offer to share my cigarette, which I've only just lit, with him. He sits with me. And we talk. He tells me about his dad, who was given a very special medal for his exploits on the Allied side during the Second World War, how he received a hero's welcome on his return home. We talk for a while about wars still being fought today, we talk about Afghanistan but I stop when I see that it's clearly filling him with genuine sadness. Eventually, I tell him of my plans to be at the G8 protests. He lowers his voice and tells me

You are free.

So here I am in Paris.

Visibly nervous. But apparently free.

Scene Twelve

He screams.

Balcony, 10th floor, Rue Vasco de Gama, Paris, 8.37pm, Tuesday 30 June, and I am freaking out

I'm supposed to be leaving tomorrow morning. I'm supposed to be hitch-hiking out of Paris to get down south to Lyon. I don't speak any French. And what's worse, the whole city is locked in by a massively complex ring road system that as a non-driver and rookie hitch-hiker, I feel completely ill-equipped to navigate. I feel trapped. Locked inside my own idiot monolingual city grid lock ring-road nightmare. And it's my own stupid fault.

Now, the balcony is about as twice as long as this space here but I can only go as far as from here to here in case my cigarette smoke gets inside. I try to stay still and calm. But mostly I pace.

It's fine. It's fine. I have friends who've done this before, it's fine. They've hitch-hiked through different parts of Europe without really knowing the language, just a few key phrases, and they've been fine, but you see those friends are actually much cooler, and braver, more adventurous, than me, I'm actually quite timid really, why did I get myself in this situation, what sort of point am I trying to prove, and to who, I'm stuck here in Paris without any reliable means of getting

He screams.

Scene Thirteen

Recorded voice:

i crawl under the paving stones

reaching for the beach beneath I stretch

squeeze pull and my belly scratches on concrete edge

people peer over the edge looking

asking where am i going and why

one speaks of pointlessness and calls me stupid

it is lost

it is a lost cause

i reach into the fresh air and salty licks my skin and soothes and cools in wind wind wind

whispers in my ears i hear a familiar loving voice 'when you do this you'll feel like you can do anything kieran'

there are people below and they seem me and they call my name and they grab my hands and pull

skin on skin and sweat mingling

an almighty heave

and i am with them

and i am glad

Scene Fourteen

An English jazz pianist, a French graphic designer and an Italian rabbi get into a car.

We're on the road out of Paris. The motorway is congested and the scooters and motorcycles whizz by, weaving in and out of the traffic with enviable agility and precision. The sun beats through the window working the car up to an oven heat.

The car is an Opel Astra Estate 1.4. The back is full of luggage, some of it spills over into the front and sits on top of us. We're sweaty, squashed in, squeezed together. This is the car that saved me.

An English jazz pianist, a French graphic designer and an Italian rabbi get into a car. A lanky Scot gets in there too. And together, they drive to Lyon.

It's not the beginning of a terrible joke, but how I did make it out of Paris and began to make real progress through the belly of Europe. Through my ridiculously fortunate encounter with a man named Gabriel. Gabriel is the English jazz pianist. He is also the driver of this car. He wears a white long-sleeved t-shirt rolled up to the elbows, pale blue faded jeans and green pumps.

This is me.
Sat next to him in the passenger seat.
Sweating.

He holds this position, before moving to become Gabriel.

Look at these people. All these cars with just one person in each. I mean, no wonder we're stuck. Imagine the congestion you'd see every day on the tube if every person moved with an invisible force-field the size of this chunk of metal around them, letting nobody else in. Clearly everything would just stop.

Gabriel was a man who needed to get from Paris, to Bologna, but decided he would fill up his car along the way with strangers he had never met, making specific stops in certain cities to drop people off, and pick up others. Gabriel driving. Me in the passenger seat.

I wish I could tell you more about this part of the journey. I wish I could tell you how Gabriel offered me a lift to Lyon saving me from my fear and anxiety in Rue Vasco de Gama. About how I thought he might leave without me, but he never did. About the people we travelled with, Ilijia, the grey bearded Italian rabbi with his fantastical imagination, incessant conversation and continual consumption of beer and cheese. About how I was supposed to only go as far as Lyon, but ended up staying in that car all the way to Bologna.

But for now, we're on the road to Bologna. The sun has settled and the air cools. Gabriel and I travel side by side, travel-weary having dropped everyone else off.

We talk for long hours freely and openly. He tells me he's going to try to find people to help me get to L'Aquila in a week or so. And he tells me about his search for an original sound. And he tells me about his decision to study jazz piano, not for the love of jazz itself but for what jazz will allow him to do.

To be able to respond completely and openly in the moment to other sounds, other influences, other rhythms, other people. You know? This is where I want to get to. And I think I can achieve it. I think you can do anything you want to and all you need are two things. The will, and honesty. And by honesty I mean being honest with yourself when you've achieved something magnificent, as well as when you fall short.

I reflect on this day we've shared. How this lift has saved me from anxiety and loneliness, and helped me across the distance of an entire country. Dropping strangers off, picking new ones up, sharing their air until we become something like friends.

As I look outside onto the Italian twilight, I remember what Gabriel said about the traffic jam on the way to Lyon. About how nothing could ever move forwards if we all lived our lives with shields around us, letting nobody else in.

I think more people should share lifts.

There'd be less cars on the road for a start.

Scene Fifteen

Kettling.

Now, I know you all know what kettling is. But, honestly, in 2009, not everyone did. I only first began to hear the word widely used after the London G20 of that year, where it was a factor in the circumstances surrounding the death of Ian Tomlinson, after the police blockaded streets, kettling the demonstration into one tight corner of the city.

This is how things must stay, I imagined. An impasse. Until things heat up and boil over, and something kicks off, with a whole arsenal of state owned weaponry poised and ready to respond. Or, perhaps things stay like this until all the protestors' enthusiasm or sense of collective purpose is squeezed out. Evaporated like steam from a kettle.

As you will see, I have my own very brief lesson in police containment strategies in this story, in Piazza Barberini, Rome, on the day of the first demonstration against the G8.

Scene Sixteen

Transition.

Video. Distance from Paris to Rome.

Music.

Scene Seventeen

In Rome I meet with someone who has kindly offered me a place to lay my head. But the apartment is small. So I set up a tent, and camp on the roof overlooking the Colosseum, and Ancient Rome.

And on my first night in Rome, I go to a Patti Smith concert.

Villa Ada, one of Rome's biggest public parks.
Monday 6 July 2009.
11pm.
It is purple. It is black. It is red. It is white. It is hot.

Patti Smith stands in front of the crowd, body swaying, arms outstretched, head tilted back.

The crowd builds, thickens with excitement.

The woman behind me shouts out yay Patti and rushes further to the front.

Look at her, Patti Smith.
The priestess of rock.
In the eternal city.
It is the eve of the first big demo against the G8.

Look at the way her long dark hair blows in the wind.

She looks tiny from here. But she feels huge.

She plays 'Dancing Barefoot'.
She plays 'Because the Night'.
She plays 'Ghost Dance'.

And now she stands in front of the crowd with her body swaying and her tilted back and her arms stretched out wide in the middle of The People Have the Power and she tells us

The people have the power to redeem the work of fools

And she tells us again

The people have the power to redeem the work of fools

And we all cheer, and we all dance

And she tells us

Use your rights

And she tells us

Take to the streets

And she tells us

Make your voice heard

And she tells us

Change is in your hands

And I want to call Pete with his muscular arms and his keen blue eyes, Pete who on the way to Knutsford services told me that fuck all changes, no matter what you do, I want to call him up and tell him

Pete, listen to this: the people have the power to redeem the work of fools. I know that now.
Do you want to know how I know, Pete?
Do you want know who told me?

Patti fucking Smith, that's who.

Scene Eighteen

Piazza Barberini, Rome.
3.30pm.
Tuesday 7 July.

This is the first major demonstration against the G8 in Italy's capital, one day before the eight leaders meet in L'Aquila. This is the event Patti Smith was talking about when she told us to take to the streets. I awoke this morning on the rooftop where I'd been sleeping to the sound of police helicopters flying low over the city. Looking down across the city streets that spiral away from the Colosseum, I could see the blue flashing lights of police cars and armoured vehicles racing towards the centre.

The people are mobilising. And Rome stirs. I anticipate something huge. I feel it in the air. This is what it's all been about.

And now I approach Barberini. Ready to join the demonstration. And –

Video. Still images from Piazza Barberini. Lines of armoured police. Anxious faces. Bored cops.

This can't be it.

This can't be what I travelled all this way to find.

Is this what Patti Smith meant, when she told us change is in your hands?

Evaporated like steam from a kettle.

I stand staring at the bored, frustrated figures and in my mind's eye I imagine each one of us, picking up a brick and charging towards the nearest bank. This image captures my imagination, and catches me off-guard, and I'm surprised to notice myself wishing it to happen.

At least we'd be doing something.

I take one long last look at Piazza Barberini and the expressionless faces that fill it before turning and leaving back down the same path I came.

Scene Nineteen

Later that evening, lying on my back while the last haze of sunlight glows through the walls of my tent, I reflect on the day in Piazza Barberini, and in particular on a conversation I had with one of the other demonstrators there, as we looked on from the sidelines, feeling alienated, and a little lost. The conversation feels important now, so I close my eyes and try to remember exactly what it was she said. And I think it was

I remember when free movement was considered a right. We say big things about democracy. We justify all manner of things in the name of democracy. But here, today, we see every effort being made to stop our voices being heard. It's like I feel, I put my body, and my voice somewhere, for a reason, for it to be heard or for it to express a concern that is of importance to us all, I think, and there is just no respect for that. For that action. And there is no attempt to listen and there is no trust. And no respect. And then what? You get like what we see today, like this static. Tension and bitterness. Where nothing moves. Just static.

Eventually I pull myself up to go and find I get the Italian news in English on the internet.

There are reports of the other demonstrations across the country today. Violence in a lot of places, particularly some horrific stuff with riot police in Turin.

Perhaps more importantly, all public access to L'Aquila has been blocked, with police declaring it a red zone. There is no public transport, and there is an armed police presence at every transport station. Even residents will have difficulty getting in.

I can't remember what I expected to find when I left my flat in Glasgow to try to get to L'Aquila, to be part of whatever it was that might be happening there. I don't know now.

But it wasn't this.

I remember the man in Paris with the yellow hat, the guy who told me

You are free

And his words ring hollow in my ears.

I begin thinking about my route home.

Scene Twenty

Recorded voice:

because it is my beloved

he tells me

that is what they do not understand

after falling beneath the paving stones i meet him and he tells me

it is my beloved

and when the person or the thing you love is in danger

you will defend it even when you are told it is a

lost cause

it is pointless

and when i think i cannot reach it i remember that i can do anything i want and all i need is two things the will

and honesty

the ground shakes rumbles and moves beneath us

our ears fill with noise

sand is thrown into the air in frenzy

structures buildings crumble and fall to the ground

there are no sirens or blue flashing lights

the earth opens up beneath our feet we tumble back, we sway,
i feel an arm around my shoulder helping

me up and slowly slowly . . .

Scene Twenty-one

He screams.

The day of the international demonstration against the G8.
Friday 10 July, 2009.
10.30am.

I'm sitting in the front seat, by the window, on a bus on its way to
L'Aquila. I didn't turn back. The bus has been organised by a big
trade union and is full of Roman student activists. I feel welcomed
by these people I'm travelling with but I'm still very much
travelling alone. I don't know these people, they don't know me,
and we don't speak each other's language.

I didn't go back though. I didn't. I found some people who'd found
a way to get there and I jumped in with them. I'm reaching my
destination. I keep telling myself this. Yes Yes Yes. I put the words
of Pete, who told me nothing changes, behind me. I put Piazza
Barberini behind me. The rows and rows of armoured cops and
frightened faces I put behind me. Back down the motorway, back
in Rome. When you do this you'll feel like you can do anything,
Kieran. We'll I'm doing it Okay? Okay. Okay. Okay. I keep telling

myself I'm okay. Until the girl sitting next to me hands me a bust card. And once again, I start freaking out.

He screams.

Now, this bust card is written entirely in English and it tells me absolutely nothing that I didn't already know. But at this moment, as we head towards L'Aquila, with all my greatest hopes and biggest fears about what I might see, or be part of when I get there, all this tumbling round my head like a drum-roll, the words from the bust card ring fresh and new and true in my ears. It says

The police can arrest you if they ask to see your identification and you refuse.

If you do show them your identification they will probably still arrest you.

Try to deter them by asking questions, thus avoiding refusing, while avoiding showing them.

Having some knowledge of Italian is crucial here.

If you are arrested make sure you are put in contact with a lawyer. Again, the ability to speak Italian will help a lot. Police who do understand English may simply pretend not to, when it suits them. There have been numerous cases of activists reporting illegal and distressing levels of abuse while under arrest after Genoa.

Make sure you are not demonstrating alone. It's much better to have a group of people who know you, who you've made plans with beforehand, and who have agreed to look out for you.

If you are alone, make sure you have a contact who you can reach if you are in trouble.

If the police charge the demonstration, hold your ground and link in with people near you. Do not panic, or try to run. Panic spreads quickly in a situation like this, and can rapidly turn to violence.

If a policeman raises his baton or gun, by law he can only use it in self-defence. However, as we all know, they can get away with doing what they please. In the case of Carlo Giuliani in Genoa, the perceived potential threat of a fire extinguisher was enough to justify a fatal bullet to his head.

Be careful.

Without hesitation I begin entering the emergency contact number into my phone. The girl next to me sees this and says to me

No, they will

She gestures throwing the phone away.

You must do this

She gestures writing on my arm.

I begin scrawling the number onto my left forearm, but by the time I'm done, the first digits are already fading, washed away by the sweat from my skin.

Scene Twenty-two

Transition.

Video. Distance from Rome to L'Aquila. Fast montage of images. Protest. Riot police. Blood. Injuries. G8 press shots. Smiling politician. Anarchist graffiti. Conflict. L'Aquila. Post-earthquake devastation. Anger.

Music.

Scene Twenty-three

The bus arrives, at the meeting point for the march, about 7 kilometres out of L'Aquila.

There is a large gathering of people already here. Black flags, red flags everywhere.

We all step off.

It is clear, and hot.

I have absolutely no idea what to do if I get separated from these people who I've only just met and who don't know me.

I try asking about the arrangements for the bus going back, but nobody seems to know, or understand what I'm saying.

I look around, unsure where to stand or what to do.

I can't go back now.

Someone from my bus brings over a big sack full of red construction site hard-hats, and empties it onto the ground. Everyone I travelled with grabs one, and they begin to write on them with anti-capitalist slogans, some in English, some Italian, and then they all put them on.

As long as I can see someone with a bright red hat on, maybe I'm okay.

Before long more and more buses arrive, and the crowd expands and grows. A van materialises from nowhere with a sound system and some sections of the crowd begin to dance. Another van with a man with a megaphone whose words I can't understand but are greeted with raucous cheers from the crowd. And we're off.

They sing, they chant, they cheer, they dance. Past the rows of armed police officers looking on from the sidelines.

As we approach L'Aquila, the remnants of the tragic earthquake become clear. Crumbling rock, broken homes, everywhere. But the people of the town stand by the side of the road and cheer us. We are here for them.

It is so, so hot.

Kieran. Kieran.

I turn round, and it is the girl from the bus.

I saw you, she says.

You look

She gestures for tired.

Here. It is for you.

She hands me a bottle of water, and I drink from it. Kieran. Kieran.

I turn again and this time two men in red hats come running towards me. I recognise them both from the bus. They give me a sticker for a campaign group that acts for the rights of the L'Aquila earthquake victims. They tell me it is a group that is organised by and for the people here. I tell them in English, we'd call that grass roots. They look at me confused. I explain that in a sense it means, like grass, it grows out from the ground from which it is born, staying true to itself, while drawing strength from neighbouring roots around it.

Yes they say, it is grass roots.

And you are our neighbour now.

We've come as far as we can go. We've reached the wall of police at the L'Aquila red zone. The helicopters overhead are lower now. Their rhythmic mechanical pulsing fills the air. But we don't care. We breathe and move together. We are pushed back, we sway. I feel a stranger's hand grip my shoulder and pull me back up. We raise our hands in peace. We raise our voices in song. And slowly, I step further, and further into the crowd.

Video. Images of the international demonstration against the G8 in L'Aquila. News footage. On-street interviews with the protestors, speaking about why they're here. One of them is **Kieran**. *He tells the interviewer: 'I have come here from Glasgow in Scotland to join with the people of L'Aquila in saying that capitalism doesn't have the answers for the economic crisis and the climate crisis that we face today, and the leaders of the world need to address these problems in new ways because the old ways have failed us.'*

Music.

End.

Beats

Kieran Hurley

Beats originally premiered at the Arches Glasgow in April 2012, before transferring to the Traverse theatre, with the following team:

Writer: Kieran Hurley
Co-director: Julia Taudevin and Kieran Hurley
DJ and sound designer: Johnny Whoop
VJ and video artist: Jamie Wardop
Technical associate: Adam Thayers

It was later remounted by Show and Tell and the Arches at the Soho Theatre and for a UK tour with Tom Searle as producer and Hushpuppy as DJ.

The writer acknowledges a debt of gratitude to Simon Reynolds, Richard Smith, Matthew Bloomer and Pulp within the imagery of the play.

Rave to the grave.

A note on the original production

Beats was orginally performed by two performers, an actor and a DJ. There was also a VJ not visible from the stage, live-mixing video footage projected throughout onto a large projector screen on the back wall. The space was filled with haze and lit with moving club lights rather than theatre lights. Sometimes Scene Two might contain ad-libbed or improvised moments in response to the mood of the audience. For the sake of this printed version, the names of the actor, DJ, VJ, and lighting operator correspond to those in the original production, but you should of course change this to fit whatever you are doing. Sometimes it has been staged as an ensemble text rather than a monologue – if you want to do that, that's great. The tracks we used in the original were as follows.

The Orb – 'Little Fluffy Clouds'
The Prodigy – 'Their Law'
Aphex Twin – 'Alberto Balsam'
Koji Kondo – 'The Legend of Zelda: a Link to the Past, Title Theme'
Aphex Twin – 'Blue Calx'

Ultrasonic – 'Annihilating Rhythm'
Aphex Twin – 'Heliosphan'
Autechre – 'Flutter'
Aztec Camera – 'Somewhere In My Heart'
Leftfield – 'Song of Life'
Josh Wink – 'Higher State of Consciousness'
Human Resource – 'Dominator'
Chemical Brothers – 'Playground For A Wedgeless Firm'
Autechre – '444'
The Prodigy – 'Weather Experience'

Scene One

What do you do when you go out, Johnno? Where do you go?

I've been hearing stories Johnno, about those boys, and about drugs. Is there something you're not telling me, son?

Feral. Out of control.

Unless stronger action is taken by the government these young people will continue to be a danger to themselves and to the rest of society.

It doesn't mean nothing. It doesn't mean nothing. It doesn't mean nothing. It doesn't mean nothing. It doesn't mean.
It means.
It doesn't mean nothing.

Scene Two

Hi.

In 1994 the Criminal Justice and Public Order Act made it illegal to have certain gatherings of people around, and this is a quote; 'music wholly or predominantly characterised by the emission of a succession of repetitive beats.'

I'm Kieran. This is Johnny Whoop. And none of this is real.

In a minute I'm going to tell you a story.

Johnny will be playing music. You are a gathering of people. The music that Johnny will be playing can for the most part be characterised by the emission of a succession of repetitive beats.

But this one isn't really real, so we're okay.

Over there are Jamie and Adam. Jamie will be live mixing some video footage like what you just saw on the screen behind me there, and Adam will control the lights. Johnny will play some music, I'll speak some words. And you'll all fill in the gaps.

This is it. This is all there is. That's your lot, really.

Which is just as well. Because nobody can arrest your imagination. Yet.

And so when I sit down there, the story will begin.

And I need you to imagine a small town in the Central Belt of Scotland, in the mid-1990s. Livingston, as it happens.

I need you to imagine bitumen pavements. And dog shit. And ten p mixes.

I need you to imagine John Major's Back to Basics campaign.

I need you to imagine a dreich evening, a row of hedges, in orange sulphur streetlight. A small street lined with pebble-dashed flats.

And I need you to imagine a boy's bedroom. Clothes on the floor. A Super Nintendo games console with the game *Zelda* on pause. A poster of the band the Stone Roses. On the floor, an empty and broken cassette case of the hit single Ebeneezer Goode by the Shamen. A faint, but noticeable smell of Lynx Africa body spray.

And I need you to imagine Johnno McCreadie.

Johnno is fifteen years old.

Small, skinny, shy, and awkward. And full to bursting of all the raw and holy emotions of a teenage boy.

His face is a canvas of plooks.

He sits in this bedroom, his bedroom, looking out the window at the dreich evening, the orange sulphur streetlight, the school across the street, the row of hedges, the bitumen pavements, the dog shit.

Johnno McCreadie, fifteen years old: disappointed with the world, and terrified of his own place in it; a still-beating heart in a concrete landscape. A moody wee shite.

Scene Three

Johnno is playing *Zelda* on the SNES for about the hundredth time. He's at that bit where you go into the Dark World for the first time and turn into a weird pink bunny rabbit. He's wearing his favourite green hoody, the one that's too big for him so when it's pulled up the hood falls right across his face, keeping him shut off from the world, separate. He'd taken to wearing it like that indoors even though in his bedroom the door to the outside world was always locked. He'd just had a lock fitted a few months ago ever since his mum had decided that: you are at an age now Johnno, where you might need a bit of, you know. Privacy.

If only she'd buy him one of those new Playstations. He's been playing this same old game for about three years now. Since he was twelve. Which is basically the same thing as forever.

Scene Four

Alison McCreadie is checking off a list. Post office. Tick. Messages. Tick. Mum's messages. Tick. Ironing.

Countdown had been on earlier when she got in, kicked off her work shoes, and started making Johnno his tea. Now it was time for that new American show, Friends.

Johnno had seemed funny. He wasn't talking. What was the problem?

She's starving. Dinner was the first thing she'd had to eat all day unless you count they two Slim Fast shakes. But she's holding out. She's no' going to let a stupid milkshake get the better of her.

She wasnae sure about that *Friends*. All squeaky voices and shiny teeth and flats with purple walls. Purple walls? Was that going to be the new thing? Good grief.

She'd been hearing things. Stories about they boys. She'd have to find a way to talk to him, find out what's going on. He'd think she was getting all worked up for nothing, but she wasn't. She wasn't.

It's no just scare stories, Johnno. You don't know it but I've seen some things myself, before you were even around. I'm no daft, son. It's not for no reason that I'm . . . ach shit.

He'd never listen. He'd never listen to all that. But she'll need to say something, she thinks, she'll need to, as she sits and ticks off a new list inside her head of all the things that her wee Johnno might get up to if he kept hanging around with that crowd.

Dogging school? Probably. Tick. Fighting? Possibly. Tick. Drinking? Seemingly. Tick. Drugs?
Tick. Tick, tick, tick, tick.

Scene Five

Call General Accident Direct on oh eight hundred one two one double oh four. You could lower your home contents and building insurance costs today.

Robert Dunlop stares at the television screen. Loads of these sortay ads on the telly noo. Probably worth looking intay, he thinks. Probably money to be saved somewhere. Who knows where to start but. Naw. Naw, no interested thanks.

You are about to experience an impressive release of power.

Oh aye. Always the same plummy Radio Four voice an aw. Was that the same guy that did aw ay these? He's probably making a racket.

The government will soon be releasing its remaining shares in National Power and Powergen.

Shares. Oh right. Probably a good idea, Robert. You've some money saved after aw.

To register, contact one of the many banks, building societies, or brokers offering a share shop service. National Power / Powergen Share Offer. The Power Issue: Share in it.

Right. Shares. Right maybe. What's this small print here, the values of shares can fluctuate any application for, ach shite. Ah well.

Privatisation Robert, really son?

But that's his Dad talking. That's exactly what his old man would have tae say, the auld idealist. Gies a break, Dad. Gies a break ya auld prick I'm forty-one. And you're deid. So get aff ma case.

He'd look into the shares thing later, he thought. Who's stopping him after aw. Naebody. Nae wife nae kids. Naebody that's who.

He chucks a couple of Pro-plus down his neck. Need to wake the system up. Been struggling for sleep since starting these night shifts. Now his old man would have recognised that as good hard work. He just hudnay ever been too keen on the fact that the hard work was being done as a member of the police force.

Ah well. Fuckum.

Later, he'd get ready to go intay the station. Later, he'd get up, heat a tin ay soup, comb his hair, prepare to leave the house. But that was later. For now, there was time for a bit more telly. He'd enjoyed that *Countdown* earlier that was always quite good. She's a good a looking woman that Carol Vorderman. Smart tae. Dunno what she's doing hanging about that Richard Whitely but. Honestly. Prick.

Scene Six

Johnno's walkman headphones dangle around his neck.

Johnno!

Mum. What does she want? He hates when she comes into his room so he unlocks the door, and steps into the hall.

Johnno what are you up to tonight? Going out later.

Out where Johnno? Just out.

What do you mean 'just out'? Dunno.

Johnno, you better not be hanging around with that Scott Smith again.

How?

Scott Smith is a bad laddie, Johnno, I've heard about him, we all hear all about him you know that fine well.

You don't even know him, Mum.

Scott Smith was Johnno's mate, but nobody called him Scott Smith. His name was Spanner. He was two years older but Johnno had been pals with him for years cos he just lived one block down the road. Johnno's mum had always been worried about Spanner leading her wee boy on to the wrong track, ever since they were wee, Johnno nine and Spanner eleven, and whenever Spanner's mum was out they'd sneak into her kitchen and drink Strongs. A Strong was when you took a glass and filled it up to the top with diluting juice, and no water. Just the concentrate stuff eh. That's a Strong. Spanner got a bad rap at school, his whole family did, but he'd always stuck up for Johnno, looked after him, and Johnno was grateful.

Johnno liked Spanner. Spanner was a good lad. So everyone else could just Fuck Off.

You don't even know him, Mum. He's alright. What happens when you go out, Johnno? Where do you go? I've been hearing stories, Johnno, about those boys, and about, about drugs. Is there something you're not telling me, son?

She was just freakin' out. All the mums were freakin' out these days, ever since all that terrible stuff over at Hangar 13 over in Ayr, and all newspaper headlines about drugs and death. It was actually, when you thought about it, quite scary. It's frustrating but. Johnno wants to talk to her about these things, he does. He wants to say, you know what, Mum, I get scared too. I do. But she doesn't understand and he doesn't have the right words to calm her down.

He sticks in his headphones and drowns out his mother's complaints.

Listen here son, you just turn that music off right away! How dare you! I am talking to you!

Johnno turns around, back into his room, and locks the door.

Right you, ya wee shite! You listen to me! Can you even hear me?

He focuses on the music, drowning out the world and his mum's voice in it. It is 'Annihilating Rhythm' by UltraSonic, it's his total favourite. That big euphoric piano line that just belongs to a world that is just not like this shitey boring shitey one that he lives and breathes. Most of all he loves the sound of the crowd. He loves how they keep in the sound of crowd. The sound of it sends a secret thrill to his stomach making him feel tiny and exposed and terrified and vulnerable and excited all at once. Kind of like the feeling he used to get when he was about ten years old and Spanner would boastfully show him those pictures of naked ladies that he kept in his bedroom. Tuning in to the sound of that cheering dancing crowd he tries to imagine that he is there with them. And pretty soon he will be.

His spine tingles. His throat tightens.

Spanner's coming round later. Spanner's coming round later in his mate's car. And for the first time ever, he's taking Johnno to an actual proper rave.

So Mum can just go and get fucked.

Before long, there are two toots on the car horn outside, Johnno stands bolt upright and still, hesitating for one second, before making a bolt for it, out the door, past his shouting mum, hood up, down the stair, and straight in to the back of Spanner's mate's car. A screech of the tyres, a shout of *awright wee man* and they're off.

Where we headed to?

Scene Seven

Robert Dunlop listens to the windscreen wipers beat their lethargic steady rhythm. The sort of the drizzle that seems in all honesty like it just can't be arsed trying.

Welcome to Motherwell. Where even the rain has given up the ghost.

Time to get out of here, move on. The commute into Glasgow was getting to be a right pain in the arse. If only he could find the time, put his mind to it, he'd get a wee place in the city. Promotion was just around the corner, he was sure of it, the extra money would help. One day, eventually, soon even, he'd move. He would.

Never one for sticking things out were you, son?

And what's that supposed to mean, Dad?

You know exactly what I mean, Robert, don't give me that.

Ach, shut it, you old fart.

Robert had lived in Motherwell his whole life. His dad, like so many others, had got a job at Ravenscraig steelworks in 1954 when the labour force expanded. When he'd finished school, a teenager, Robert had joined the same workforce at first. A steelman, just like his old man. He was there during the strikes in 1980 after the Tories got in, he was out there picketing, leafleting, the lot. He was into all that stuff once, just like everyone else was, we all go through it. Except you couldnae let it alone could you, Dad?

We won then, son. We won in 1980.

Things were changing though, Dad. Things were changing and had you to keep up. You knew it yourself. You said when they went after the miners, you said it would be us next.

I always said we should have supported the miners. If we had then maybe

Maybe nothing. You saw the way it was going. You're supposed to get wise as you get older, Dad. You're supposed to get sensible. If you want to help your community you find a more practical way of doing it.

Like joining the police force, you mean?

Well exactly. Fucking exactly. Linwood. Bathgate. Gartcosh. Ravenscraig.
Monuments to an old way of thinking. Those old certainties were dying, Dad, just like you were, and you knew it even back then.

It's called solidarity, Robert. Solidarity. Togetherness. The sort of mentality that says, see me and you, we're the same. What's good for you is good for me. A sort of collective empathy. That's what they were trying to destroy, son.

It's called pissing into the wind, Dad. There was to be no stopping it.

You're no listening, that's no the point. It was a fight for an understanding of who we are, of what we are. Of what we should be.

And if you want to know who won that fight, Dad, take a look around. Maybe if you'd still been here to see it all finally come crashing down you'd have understood. It's pointless trying to imagine anything beyond the facts of what you can see around you. Scorched earth, Dad. Scorched fucking earth.

It had been two years since the plant was demolished. He tunes into the radio. Some news thing. Seemed that constant background noise was necessary these days to get a bit ay fucking peace.

Some believe that unless stronger action is taken by the government these young people will continue to be a danger to themselves and to the rest of society. If the proposed Criminal Justice Bill becomes law it will grant police and local authorities increased powers to shut down these 'raves' which many are increasingly seeing as an anti-social problem. But don't young people have a right to party? And if the government is allowed to restrict their civil liberties, might not ours be next?

Aye, thinks Robert. A wee place in the city. That'd be nice. Somewhere in the country maybe. Maybe get a dog. Something like that.

Scene Eight

They've been driving for a couple of hours now.

It wasn't supposed to be this far away.

Spanner's mate, the driver, is called something like Dennis or Derek, but Johnno has completely forgotten his actual name already due to his own insistence on calling himself the D-Man, or D-Day, or D-Funk, or D-Mob, or D-Dog, or D-Bomb, or other combinations of his own first initial and a seemingly randomly selected noun.

D-Person is trying to act like everything is cool, while Spanner gets increasingly irate. Johnno, trying to hide his growing nerves, stays quiet. And still.

What do you mean you're sure? How sure is sure?

Listen geeza we're on the right track now I'm telling ya.

D-Guy was seemingly from somewhere in the south of England, though Johnno had been unable to engage him in normal conversation for long enough to find out what exactly he was doing in Livingston.

Call the number. Call the number again.

From where, you think I just carry a phone around like some yuppy?

Stop at the next services, use a fuckin' payphone or sumhin, here, fuckin, gie me the number, an' fuckin', I'll dae it.

Spanner had explained to Johnno how it worked. He had a mate, presumably the D-Laddie here, who in turn had a mate who knew someone who worked in a record store in Glasgow where you would go to pick up the number for this big free party happening out of town. All you had to do was call that number and they'd tell you exactly where it was.

It's all about keeping it on the down-low, Spanner had said. You game for it wee man? It'll be proper. The whole plan is in place eh an nuhin can possibly go wrong.

And what you gonna say to them exactly: excuse me mate I'm at a service station off the motorway in the arse end of fucking nowhere – you heard of it by any chance? Can you give me directions from there? We already know where it is you twat.

Well how are we no there yet then?

We missed the turning and now we're going back I'm telling ya, I'm fucking on top of it alright! Tunes, we need some fucking tunes.

Spanner fiddles with the radio tuner.

And if the government is allowed to restrict their civil liberties, might not ours be next?

Not that for fucksake!

D-Baws fumbles around for a tape he likes and thrusts it into Spanner's hand, who resentfully slams it in and hits play.

They sit. Listening. Johnno pipes up.

What . . . what is this?

This my son, is Autechre. You like it? Put on sumhin a bit more bouncin man

No, I, like it, it's, it's . . . different . . . it's cool.

Yes mate, listen to that beat yeah . . . Criminal Justice And Public Order Bill. You know about this yeah?

Johnno nods, although in truth he's not quite sure.

What they are trying to do yeah is outlaw raves. Criminalise the party scene yeah. So what they're saying they want to do is make it illegal to have a big outdoor party with, and this is a quote, music characterised wholly or predominantly by the emission of a succession of repetitive beats. Yeah? So Autechre, what they did yeah, was they recorded this track where no bars contain identical beats. This track has no, by definition, no repetitive beats. You could have a big fuck off party and listen to nothing but this track and they'd have to let ya! It'd be totally fucking legal and they'd have to fucking let ya!

Aye it'd be pure murder but.

Shut up, Spanner. This is what I'm talking about yeah, it's like music as a political act. They try to persecute us but we become radical by necessity!

Oh for fucksake will you gie at rest ya wally?

Fuck off Spanner, listen to the D-Boy! What I'm saying is yeah like rock n' roll and the music of our parents' generation, it was all narrative and linear, and icon hero worship but this, this is different. This about a pulse yeah, it's a living thing, a living pulse, yeah, and they can't kill it.

It's a fuckin' tune! A record! No even a very good one. Aws it is is, it doesnae mean . . . nuhin. Nuhin. Awright? Noo let's just get to this fuckin' party, an fuckin', get on wi' it. For fucksake!

It doesn't mean nothing? It doesn't mean nothing! You need to radicalise yourself Spanner. You hear me? Radicalise yourself mate. Radicalise!

Shut. The Fuck. Up!

And so it continued. Johnno had stopped listening, he didn't really understand what Spanner's weird mate was on about anyway. A living pulse. Whatever. Instead he tunes in to this new music, willing it to calm his apprehensive heart. A living pulse. He focuses on that soft repetitive melody, and as he stares at his own shady reflection in the window he begins to imagine that melody as his own living pulse. Visualising it like liquid flowing through his veins. And he imagines it as the living pulse of the tarmac, and the electricity pylons that flick past his eyes keeping time. And of the streaky beads of rain catching and refracting the sparkle of passing headlights as they slide along the window, clinging on to the glass for dear life.

Scene Nine

Fucksake, Johnno. Fucksake.

Maybe she should just go to bed. No. No, she should wait up.

Fuck.

She fiddles with radio.

these 'raves' which many are increasingly seeing as an anti-social problem. But don't young people have a right to party? And if the government is allowed to restrict their civil liberties, might not ours be next?

No. Not that. That's not what she wants to listen to at all, shite, change it. What else is there? Best of the Eighties? Fuck. Best of the Eighties it is. Okay. Shit.

Young people have a right to and for this and that. She never had a right. She was pretty sure nobody ever asked her about her rights.

Lists. Where were her lists? Ironing. Okay. Might as well get started on the bloody ironing.

The wee shit.

She'd really, really tried to make the world that he came into a safe one, and a happy one, and one that he could be thankful for and it's no perfect alright. Alright Johnno? It's no perfect but it was hard bloody work just to keep things ticking over, without you running off and making it look like I cannae even cope, and this is the fucking thanks . . .

The things she should do when she sees him. Ground him. Tick.

Slap him. Tick.

Scream.

Oh she could scream. But she doesn't. She just stands behind the ironing board. Rooted. Frozen. As still as furniture.

The song on the radio is Aztec Camera's 'Somewhere In My Heart'.

It's no' perfect this, but it was the best I could do. And it's all I've got, just this wee flat and you. Son.

Batter him. Tick. Strangle him. Tick. Hug him.

Just, hug him.

Tick. Tick, tick, tick, tick.

In a wee living room, in a tiny flat in Livingston, clutching a clothes iron firmly in her left hand and staring at the pattern on the wallpaper, wide-eyed and empty-stomached, while on the radio some young men from East Kilbride sing about walking down love's motorway, singing hearts and flowers, and a star above the city in the northern chill. Standing there, completely still, Alison McCreadie thinks about her son. And for the first time in years, she begins to cry.

Scene Ten

At some point up the road as the bickering continues, the D-Man takes what he hopes is the right turning, and slows down as they come into a small country road in suspiciously heavy traffic.

This looks like sumfink.

The slow traffic comes to a sudden standstill. Someone up ahead has stopped for a piss. Other male passengers, having presumably been driving some distance too, see the window of opportunity and hurl themselves through it, and they all follow suit. A winding line of traffic at a standstill pierced by multiple simultaneous arcs of silvery uriney gold in the moonlight, like a punctured garden hose.

Spanner looks around. Lads. We're in the right place.

D-Bag lets out a big laugh and starts rhythmically pumping the car horn and banging his head to his own beat.

And so they arrive.

It's dark where they dump the car but they can hear noise and see some kind of tent thing up ahead. It looks smaller, and a bit shiter, than the ones Johnno's heard about. The ground is damp and muddy and the air is cold. They're about to start heading over when Johnno feels Spanner warmly take his hand.

Here. You'll need one ay these.

Spanner takes his hand away. Johnno looks down at his own palm and sees a big round white pill with a picture of something that looks like a star cut into it. He looks back up to Spanner, who is smiling.

Are you taking one?

Am takin' one aye. I've got another for later if you want.

Johnno is silent.

Dinnae listen to the scare stories fae school, Johnno, eh. You're fine. It's fine. Mostly, see when sumhin bad happens it's just cos ay the water. Just cos ay drinkin' too much water. Go easy on the water and you'll be fine.

Like a Strong?

What?

Eh, like a Strong. Remember. When we used to fill up a glass with diluting juice, and no water. A Strong. It's better if you go easy on the water, it's more . . . fun.

. . . Aye. Aye, like a Strong. Nice one Johnno. Cool.

Johnno looks at his hand again. But this isn't like a Strong though. This isn't even like the time Spanner got detention for crushing up the blackboard chalk and snorting it up his nose. This is it.

He looks around at the mud and grass, and feels a chill around his cheeks as he stares forwards at the unspectacular and uninviting tent up ahead. It'll never be like it was, that's what they always said. All those magazines that Spanner lent him always said the raving scene is over, it's sold out and moved on, it's not the same, it's in the past now, it's changed. It's been done.

But it's not been done by me.

Everyone's always talking about the past and saying that right now is shite. Just empty and shite. And they're probably right too. But what's left then? What's left for me?

Fuck it.

Fuck the lot ay them.

Scene Eleven

Johnno feels nothing at first.

They're skirting round the edges of the dancing crowd in the tent. Johnno feels out of place, uncovered, like he's come wearing the wrong clothes to the school dance.

Maybe Spanner's been done. Maybe someone's sold him a paracetamol or something. That'd be just like him eh. That'd be just like the thing. The relief at the thought outweighs the disappointment.

Are you sure these are real Spanner?

Course they're fuckin' real, just gie it a minute.

*

Scorched earth, Dad. Scorched fucking earth.

These words still echo in Robert's mind as he steps through the doors of Finnieston police station, and the Super says to him: it's been a while since you've hud tae use your storm trooper gear eh PC Dunlop?

Aye, it is aye.

Still mind your riot control training alright? Aye, aye I do, aye.

Well. Just as fucking well.

*

These are never real, Spanner. You've been done ya dick. Fuckin' paracetamol or something I bet ye.

Fuckin' shut it Johnno. You'll see.

And then. Sure enough.

The rush sneaks up on him. It starts with a sort of fuzzy jelly warm ache in the legs and the torso and before spreading up the back of the neck like an electric waterfall flowing backwards, mainlining to his brain. He feels like he might fall over, like he might throw up at any moment but it's still, glorious. Feeling like he needs to sit down he leans into Spanner who puts his arm round him.

Are you alright, mate?

Johnno looks up at his friend, a weird conspiratorial smile cracking across his face. He breathes out loudly and pulls him in for a hug, a warm glow pulsing through his body, a sort of blissful golden effervescence like he's got champagne for blood. His mate, his best mate squeezes his body tight and starts to laugh. Glorious. Fucking glorious.

Holy shit Spanner man, holy fuck. Fuck.

Spanner keeps laughing and so does Johnno and for a while they both just stand there holding each other and laughing. D-Guy who has been watching the dancing crowd with a kind of desperate impatience turns round and noticing instantly what has happened throws his hands behind his head and shouts out yeeeeeeessss and lunges towards them. To Johnno's surprise he starts massaging their necks with each of his hands, big smile beaming. Johnno loves it but. The massage. The touch. He really really loves it.

*

Robert surveys his equipment:

Helmet – check

Steel-capped boots – check, body armour – check

Harness, including radio, cuffs, CS spray – check

Baton – check

Safe. It's aw designed to make you totally safe.

He feels strangely outside of his own body. Robert. You're safe.

Just some kids. Just some daft kids having a party in a field. I mean, aw this, seems a bit much really doesn't it.

Aye it does, Robert, aye it bloody well does. Fuck off, Dad, naebody asked you.

*

Weaving in and out of dancing bodies they make their way into the crowd, passing the faces of all the dancers, kids like them, older folks who look like they work in an office or could be a younger teacher, girls with dreadlocks like Johnno's never seen, all together moving, every one ensnared in the rhythm, their faces some contorted, lost in music, but each one fucking beautiful. They catch his eye and he feels he understands them. He feels them see him. A gleeful, fleeting, wordless, exchange: welcome son. Welcome.

And without even noticing the music finds a flow through him, speaking straight to his body. Like it's flowing through him but like he's immersed in it at the same time, engulfing him in its immediacy, in its intimacy. And the rushing stops and he locks into a groove and hits a blissful plateau, his own body a tiny brick in a wall of sweating muscle, for hours. Hours. Slipping effortlessly between individual interactions and a sort of tribal mass consciousness. All of us, he thinks. All of us, right now, together, here! Knowing that the world outside these walls is just a cold cruel shite-hole, but fuck it cos the only thing that really counts for anything is now! Us! Here and now!

*

You ready for some action then?

Robert rubs his sweaty hands on the rough, thick, tough canvas of his blue overalls and looks up at the officer opposite him.

Aye uh huh.

Show the wee scumbags who the fucking boss is.

Super says it's precautionary. What was that?

Precautionary measure

What?

Oh, eh. Nothing.

*

Johnno's sense of time and space is lost. Could be five minutes or an hour since he last saw Spanner. But he's never felt less alone and so he's not scared. Not scared one bit.

Some water wee man?

No, had enough thanks. Go easy on the water. It's more fun without it. Like a Strong right. Like a fucking Strong, eh?

*

Robert clenches his teeth.

The squad are laughing slapping backs, psyching up for the bust.

His throat dries and tightens.

Has anyone eh, has anyone got a drink ay water?

*

I love you man I mean it. I really love you.

Where's Spanner. Who's Spanner? Aw he's my mate. He's my mate, have you seen him?

All of us holding on together, eh. I fucking love you, man.

It doesn't mean nothing, that's what he said. He said it doesn't mean nothing. But it does but. It is real. It fuckin' is though. Well but what if we just pretend that it's real. Imagine. Imagine that it is. What then? What would we have then, eh?

Fucking hell you're tripping, wee man.

*

Radios crackle. Orders are given. Briefings are made.

We have tried to move them on peacefully but there has been resistance.

Resistance? What kind of resistance? Well. They've had their chance. Okay. Well.

They're breaking the law, well. We are the law. They're breaking the law and they're refusing to stop.

We're here to keep things right, make sure everyone's, kept, safe.

Well then. Fucking well then! Let's go! Let's fucking do this!

*

Spanner? Have you seen Spanner?

Johnno staggers exhausted and weak at the knees, to pause for a moment to catch his breath. In his misty consciousness he feels a tremor through the crowd. A panic, a fear. His body is tossed around as the crowd begins to scatter. He forces his body through the crowd, propelling forwards in aimless manic, physical hysteria.

*

Get back! Get back! Get back! Get back!

Robert hears these words come tumbling out his mouth like they're being said by someone else.

The crowd begins to scatter. Scattering like dogs.

Feral. Out of control.

Some of them try to push back. To fight back. Adrenalin courses through his veins, his own animal instincts kicking in.

It's fight or flight. Fight or fucking flight, right?

Out of the corner of his eye he sees a figure in a green hoody charging towards him. In one instant trained reflex he reaches for his baton and raises it high above his head–

The last thing Johnno is aware of before the weapon comes crashing down, is the sudden sight of a row of shields, of stamping boots, charging, shouting, beating, and a voice ringing in his ears screaming: POLICE.

Scene Twelve

Where, is, he?

Scene Thirteen

Jesus fuck.

Johnno hurts. In every way, he hurts.

He looks around at the rows of dejected souls, gurning jaws, confused and frightened faces; ghostly white skin, pasty and damp and reptilian.

Those wide gaping eyes which once looked so mighty and angelic now just look desperate, childlike and lost, like the panicked dead eyes of fish flapping out of water, under the cold neon strip lights of the Finnieston police station foyer.

Fucking hell. I know how these munters feel.

The pain of the beating throbs dull and warm in the side of his face and deep in his shoulders. He shivers.

Later, much, much later, when his body has grown and changed, sitting at home while the television shows a mass of young people, students, breaking into Millbank tower and an onscreen voice argues that they can't be allowed to run around wild, they need to be taught a lesson, John McCreadie, thirty-one years old will become suddenly aware of an echo through his muscles, a brief pain in his right shoulder. And for the first time in years he'll remember sitting in the police station foyer feeling vulnerable, lost, deeply alone, and quite, quite scared.

But that's later. Much, much later.

Oh fuck fuck fuck. His bones feel like they could turn to dust, his throat is parched, he wants to be sick but there is nothing inside. What happens now?

I've been hearing stories, Johnno, about those boys.

Aye, Mum.

That Scott Smith is a bad laddie, Johnno. You don't even know him, Mum.

Wanting nothing more than to crawl into somewhere warm and make the whole bright, hostile, world just disappear he pulls his green hoody up tight around his ears, clenches his eyes tight shut, and tries, to focus on, to remember, what he was doing before aw this. Before he followed that fucking dafty Spanner down this rabbit hole of shite.

Zelda. He was playing fucking *Zelda.*

If this was *Zelda* right now, he'd know exactly what to do, he'd know every right turn, every secret passageway that you need to escape the dungeon. If this was *Zelda,* he'd even know about a secret door that leads to a special treasure chest. And you'd open it, the treasure chest and there would be a wee red heart inside. And you'd grab it, the heart, and that would make your health go up. He pictures a broken, empty, shell of a heart filling up to the top till it glows hot, and bright, and red. He could use some of that action the now. A total fucking beezer.

Zelda V: The Adventures of Johnno – an illegal rave fairytale!

He breathes in deep. And opens his eyes.

Fuck.

Scene Fourteen

Spanner wakes up, face down in mud, with his T-shirt caked in his own sick.

Fucksake man aw naw.

Johnno? Johnno where are ye? Ya wee dick.

Fuck am ah outside fur? Fuck's happenin here man aw naw

Later it'll begin to come back to him. The drive oot, the party, getting separated fae wee Johnno. The polis arriving, the mad bolt for it when the crowd turned nasty, escapin' doon the road an keepin' the party goin wi two, was it two lads fi, fuck knows, in the back ay a van somewhere and must ay stumbled back up the road tay. . . here.

Just ootside the D-Man's motor. Tidy.

Later still, in a week or so, when he sees wee Johnno after school, he'll hear aboot how the wee man got knocked aboot by the fuzz. Got a blow tae the cheek fae the butt ay a stick like that – doosh – and then another swipe – wap – like that back across the shooders. He'll see Johnno's bruises and he'll look at the wee man a wee bit different. Sort ay impressed, eh. But wi a sort ay, sadness an aw, for sumhin, lost. Mibbe. He'll hear aboot how Johnno got taken tae a station an how he pure shat it cos he thought he was in for it but how they'd actually just called his maw who came and picked him up but by the sounds ay hings that had actually been the worst bit. He'll hear aboot how Johnno's maw says that if she ever sees the two ay them hingin aboot thegither ever again she'll fuckin' actually kill the baith ay thum so noo they've got tay be pure sly aboot hingin aboot noo. Later on, eh. Later on he'll find out aw ay this.

Because right now the only things in the whole world that Scott Spanner Smith knows about are the bright morning light, the freezing cold air, the deep aching pain of body and soul, and the cold, bitty remains of yesterday's Pot Noodle stuck behind his teeth.

Scene Fifteen

Robert's left eye twitches slightly, as his hands grip the steering wheel. There were no too many problems. The Super had said that was a good bust. Textbook.

His bleary eyes blink in the daylight. He'd forgotten how long it took for the adrenalin to leave the system.

There was this kid. This wee laddie. Looked only about fifteen. Robert had seen him, sitting there in the station, green hoody too big for him pulled up, wee bony face poking out, eyes shut. Purple bruise across the side of his cheek. He'd seen him, and he'd recognised him. He recognised him from the bust.

And he had stood, unable to take his eyes off the kid, as he remembered: a swift blow down with the butt, a swipe across the back. Two beats. Textbook.

The boy was dripping in sweat and looked, so, light, so fragile. But, other-worldly, almost. Serene. What did he know that Robert didn't?

He recognised him, aye, but this was the first time, he knew, that he'd really seen him.

Later, years later, when Robert Dunlop is still commuting from Motherwell and any real thoughts of significant promotion have disappeared into the rear view mirror as he edges his way towards retirement; when this brief encounter with the green hooded boy is left obscured under the gathering dust of decisions, and convictions, ground out over a lifetime, Robert will come to remember Johnno quite differently. He'll remember seeing a savage, unruly youth. A hooligan. A yob.

But that was later. Much, much later. What are they playing at these kids, eh?

They're a danger to themselves. Out of control. Was never like that in my day. It's a disgrace, really, it's, it's disruptive to local communities is what it is, it's, no right.

Robert. What is it you're so afraid of, son?

Fuck off, Dad! You cannae just let them run around wild. Okay? Come on, they need to learn! They need to be taught a lesson, or else what will we have?

Or else what will have.

He glances into the rear view mirror.

Anyway. Must remember to look intay they shares. National Power and Powergen wasn't it. Probably stop at the chemists an aw pick up something to help me sleep.

Fucking night shifts man.

I could really use a good night's rest.

Scene Sixteen

Johnno folds his bruised and aching frame deep into the corner of the back seat of his mum's car.

What. A. Downer.

Alison stares straight ahead. Determined no to make eye contact in the rear view mirror. Determined no to let him off the hook, determined to make him feel as terrible, as helpless as she had done.

She sneaks a glance.

Look at him. Swollen face, what had they done to him?

She clenches her teeth, and flicks on the indicator switch. Tick, tick, tick, tick . . .

Johnno, not daring to look up at his mum, stares out the window at the passing streets as they make their way on to the motorway.

Men in suits, bankers maybe, aggressively commanding the pavements on their way to work.

An old man lying on a bench, covered in newspapers.

A street corner with three different bookies on it with their shutters down.

And onto the motorway, a cavalcade of concrete, petrol and steel, carrying hundreds of different people, different lives, along in the same direction, passing each other out, never noticing as they sail by in their individual little pods.

Shut off from the world, separate.

This is it. This is all there is. That's your lot, really.

But that was Spanner talking surely. Where was he? He'd be fine. He'd managed worse, Johnno was sure.

He watches the early morning sun reflecting off the passing road signs. Bouncing repetitive rays of light, momentarily cross the inside of his mum's car, catching her cheekbone, his hand, the metal piece on that seatbelt. A fleeting glimmer.

He feels a tingle through the back of his neck. Was that residual drugs in his bloodstream, the morning cold, or, what? And almost before his mind can catch up he feels his body remembering, and imagining.

And he imagines huge, pulsating crowds. He imagines a tingle in his spine.

He imagines an electric waterfall.

And he imagines, and remembers, togetherness; a sort of collective empathy and see me, see you, we're the same, what's good for you is good for me, I'm for you, so welcome son. Welcome.

Later, when he sees him next week after school, he'll try to explain all this to Spanner and Spanner will tell him that he's an arsehole, that it's no real. The drugs fast track the chemicals that produce all that stuff to trick you. That's why it ruins your brain, that's why you feel like shite for so long after. You're using up all of next week's happiness in one night.

But that's later.

Right now, staring out at the bleakness of the urban morning Johnno keeps his eyes wide open this time and lets it all play out against his weary retina. Speeding over the concrete river of the motorway he sees the world, his world at the close of the twentieth century, and he sees himself in it. He feels a flickering warmth inside his cold, exhausted body. A tiny glow. An empty heart shell, fills up, throbbing bright and red and hot. A living pulse. It beats and beats and beats and beats and beats and beats and beats.

He looks up at his mum, and bravely, hopefully, tries to catch her eye.

Later, back at home, when she's helping Johnno painfully lift up his arms to remove his green hoody, Alison will softly run her fingers along the purple bruises across the top of his back. He'll take her hand, and say: it's okay, Mum. I'm okay.

She'll look at him, and say: I know. But that's later.

As the world flickers past the window Johnno thinks about home; the familiar streets, the school building that he can see from his bedroom window. But he imagines something else as well. Something beyond the facts of what he can see around him. Beyond the bricks and mortar of his school, the bitumen roads, the orange sulphur streetlights, the dog shit. An idea. An understanding of who we are, of what we are. Of what we could be.

And he holds on to it. Because nobody can arrest his imagination.

Sitting in the back seat of his mother's car, with her staring straight ahead refusing to look at him, refusing to talk to him, wanting to scream at him but secretly, underneath it all just deeply, deeply glad that he's alive, sitting there with his head aching and his body sick and weak and broken, with his blood flowing dirty through his veins, with his eyes wide open and his bruised cheek pressed hard against the cold glass, Johnno McCreadie, fifteen years old, green hoody and spotty skin, sits turning the same phrase over and over and over in his head. A small smile melts across his weary face.

It doesn't mean nothing. It doesn't mean nothing. It doesn't mean nothing. It doesn't mean nothing. It doesn't mean nothing. It doesn't mean nothing. It doesn't mean nothing. It doesn't mean nothing. It doesn't mean nothing. It doesn't mean nothing. It doesn't mean nothing. It doesn't mean nothing. It does *not* mean *nothing*.

Heads Up

Kieran Hurley

Heads Up first premiered at Summerhall at the Edinburgh Festival Fringe 2016, produced by Show And Tell and with the following team:

Writer and performer: Kieran Hurley
Co-directors: alex swift and Julia Taudevin
Music and sound: MJ McCarthy
Lights: Malcolm Rogan
Dramaturgy: Liam Hurley

Produced by Show and Tell. Script developed with support from the Playwrights' Studio Scotland. Produced with support from the Tron Theatre, Glasgow. Part of the Made In Scotland showcase.

A note on the original production

Heads Up was originally performed by one performer, sat a desk, with sound operated live onstage using a pair of audio samplers that were constantly operated throughout.

A room. A chair. A desk.

On the desk, a microphone, two audio samplers and an unlit candle.

Kieran *enters. He is wearing a suit. He is wearing no shoes. He sits. He lights the candle. He speaks.*

Hello.

This is a story about the end of the world.

It is a story about a city. Like this one.

Here and now.

It is a story about me. And it is a story about you.

It begins, as it ends. With a breath.

An audible in-breath.

*

You hold on tight to the air in your lungs as the glass-walled elevator pulls away to Floor 22; the city streets rushing from you as you push up, up, up.

You step into the marble corridor. Your shoes make an expensive-sounding click.

You are Mercy. That is your name. The approving blue light of the security scanner tells you so as you press your finger to its cold glass, the heavy door to your office yielding obediently. Mercy, you have moulded yourself in the image of this world, wearing its clothes like armour, contorting your being in order to fit. And now you fit.

Your leather seat welcomes you, knowing your shape. The contents of your desk lie before you; tidy, neat, pleasing. Keyboard. Monitors. Phone. Your favourite gold fountain pen. The picture frame with the Bible quote from your mum. The God stuff means nothing to you, you just like the words: 'And I will show wonders in the heavens above and signs on the earth below.'

Your colleagues – white blokes all – have desks bedecked with motivational phrases like 'Go The Extra Mile.' You smile, knowing that none of them have ever truly had to go an extra mile for anything in their lives, the silly tits.

You know how much they resent you. You feel it through the walls, but you don't care. It's another driver.

Someone once joked that if the markets are God then you are a high priestess. You didn't laugh. You know the mystical force of the confidence trick, the enchanted numbers, the illusory words with such real effects in this flesh world. You deal in Futures. It's what you do.

You read the signs, detect patterns. Watching, analysing, reporting. Last month you had spotted fluctuations in crop values due to unprecedented floods from which you could predict for the shareholders a sharp price hike on rice. So everyone stockpiles rice.

Holds on to it. Then sells it for more in the future. The future is where it all happens. The future is where all the money is made. Growth, debt, everything all of this is built on, just a deal we make between ourselves now and an imagined future moment.

To deal in Futures, you tell yourself as you take a deep breath in and steady your mind for the task in hand, is to deal directly in the magic, and the spell of capital.

You don't eat at work because hunger is a natural aid to productivity. You have not slept in days. You're too well aware of the close cousinly relationship between crisis and opportunity, of how these corridors have been lately fizzing with the thrill of global catastrophe. National bonds nose-diving with the escalating migrant crisis; collapsing currency triggering a new potential housing crisis; mass investment in military technology in response to the global climate crisis; crises within crises within crisis crisis crisis.

A dying bee twitches and crawls its way across your desk. On the twenty-second floor, you think, that's weird. You crush it with the butt of your pen. The sound and the feeling makes the skin on the back of your neck tighten. But they're dangerous when they're dying. You sweep it to the floor. You focus. You breathe. You get to work.

*

You curl up in your seat, tuck your tiny feet under your legs and chew on what's left of the nail of your thumb. You're looking at a screen. On the screen is a map of land. Of a city.

The map of the city moves. It moves before your eyes, in crude graphics. In the top right-hand corner of the screen the name: ASHVILLE. You'd named it after yourself. You. You are Ash.

You're playing *Sim City* on a PC SNES emulator that you downloaded about two years ago and basically forgot about.

You like playing the old games. You dunno. It's cause they're sort of stupid and funny and you dunno, you just like them. Even though your mum's really worried that everyone thinks you're weird.

Girls play computer games, Mum, it's a thing now yeah? Jesus.

You wrap your duvet warm around your shoulders, your baggy pyjama clothes clinging to you like an extra skin.

You'd built it so that there were no roads in Ashville. Because when there were roads you got all these issues with traffic congestion and pollution that you had to fix. So you have realised that it's best if you just don't have any roads obviously. You could just have train tracks and that was fine. Matthew always said it was stupid to just have train tracks because that would never work in real life.

But this isn't real life is it Matthew? It's *Sim City* for the Super Nintendo from the fucking olden days. Cunt.

You hate him. Matthew. You hate him even though you can't stop thinking about him.

You set the tax at seven. That was about the right setting for tax. Seven. Definitely no higher than eight.

You don't think it feels like a fair reason to be dumped. Matthew had said that now that you were both nearly thirteen it was fair enough for him to get to touch your fanny.

It's not that you don't want him to touch your fanny. Maybe you do, in fact, want him to touch your fanny. Maybe.

You just didn't want him to be such an arsehole about it. Other boys were shy about that stuff still.

You'd told him to go and fuck off so then he'd dumped you for being tight. And then he sent that picture round that you'd sent him before.

The stupid bastard fuck.

You smell bacon fat and vegetable oil, rising up from downstairs, filling your nostrils.

You hear your mum calling. It's time to go to school. No escaping it.

You remember there's a thing where you could send in disasters. To destroy everything you'd built. All the hours of careful Ashville city planning, growing it all up. You could just massacre it with a click. Built into the game. Like a fun option. You look at the options. The options are tornado, earthquake, flood, plane crash, boat crash and the Godzilla thing.

You click the Godzilla thing.

Residential zones, crunch!

Commercial zones, crunch!

Casino, crunch!

Mayor's house, crunch!

Police station, crunch!

School, crunch!

Ha!

Fucking Matthew cunt.

*

You watch a moving image of yourself in a giant room full of light and sound, singing in front of thousands of other humans, reaching for you, screaming, reaching.

The video on the laptop stalls. Then buffers. Then plays again. You watch your singular form traverse the enormous empty stage in front of giant white letters spelling out your name in bright lights: LÉON. You.

You are the only person in the world who could be subject to such emotional mistreatment.

A long line of cocaine arrives. You hoover it up.

You pause the video.

See? You say. You see? There are people out there who *need* me.

You watch as the people in the room all nod. Another line. You offer it to the room. Does anyone want one? Does anyone want some of this? The people in the room shake their heads and look at their feet. No? Really? Okay.

You declare to the room: some of us are born to take risks. Not many of us but some. It's a cross we have to bear. And I don't have time for this, okay? If they're not going to nominate me that's their problem. *I* am the artist. *They* are the shitheads.

The people in the room nod. They say: of course.

Even if they didn't like the fucking actual album, at least a nod of recognition. For the humanitarian work, you know! Fuck!

Your manager speaks. He says: Your girlfriend.

Everyone sure they don't want any? Sure? You wish that someone wanted some.

A contract arrives. You are told to sign it. You sign it.

The TV is showing a programme about bees. You remember reading about the poor endangered bees. It was so totally unfair what was being done to the bees. You empathise with the bees. You tell the room: we have to do something about the bees! Someone writes down: do something about the bees.

You tell the person writing, you tell him: what's your name?

He says: Jeff. Jeff, you say. Jeff. Would you like to join me in some coke, Jeff? Please? Jeff shakes his head. Your manager speaks. He says: Léon! Your girlfriend –

A phone rings. You answer. It is your publicist. He tells you: stay off Twitter! You tell him: fuck off.

You tell the room: we are gonna save the bees! Get the word out! Quick! Tell the *NME*. Tell *Rolling Stone*. Tell *Mix Mag*! Jeff, get me the BBC. Tell them we're on our way over with an exciting – no a fucking *pivotal* announcement. Something's gotta be done or we're all fucked and it's not the fucking bees' fault is it Jeff? Someone's gotta do something and it looks like it's got to be me.

Why must it always have to be you? But there are people, there is a planet out there which needs you.

Someone asks: does this mean we're dropping the ice-caps thing now then?

You declare to the room: the planet needs me!

Your manager speaks. He says: your girlfriend!

You say: what. Yes. What. What is it?

He says: your girlfriend is in labour.

What? Which one? Amy?

Yes, Amy, the fucking pregnant one.

Now? You ask him. Fucking now. But there's so much to be done! Now? Fucking now?

Yes. He tells you. Now. She's in labour now. Fucking now!

*

You will be enthusiastic
You will have initiative
You will work at pace
You will not blame others
You will not become flustered when the heat is on
You will not do things only for show
You will not wait to be told
You will not be here simply for the money
You will love the coffee and the snacks that you serve

The streetlight outside your window fills the room in headache glow. Your face is pressed defiantly against the pillow. Your eyes resolutely shut. The light glows through the skin of your eyelids, a warm bloody orange. Extra streetlamps, they said. For new CCTV, they said. To make the neighbourhood safe, they said. Sure.

You squint open your eyes. Next to your mattress, on the floor, you see: your hairnet and name tag from work. It says: Abdullah. You.

You had been visited at work last week by mystery shoppers. Undercover monitoring of employees. To ensure people-perfect behaviour. Everyone who passes through the branch is supposed to leave feeling good. All the staff are meant to provide an emotional role not just a functional one. You know this. If the report shows people-perfect behaviour it's good because everyone gets a bonus. If someone falls short, nobody gets a bonus, everyone gets a warning, and the report says whose fault it was.

On the day of the mystery test, you'd had no breakfast. Debt repayments had meant you had to skip the weekly shop. As you walked the long walk into town in the rain with your hoody up you had been stopped and questioned by police, no reason. Just how it is. The next day, the report came in. You had been less than people-perfect.

You had said to your manager: please. You had said: I need this job.

The report with your name on it had been stuck to the staff room wall. You had been given one more chance.

You will cope well with pressure
You will be a role model

You will never give up
You will always do your best
You will admit your mistakes
You will go the extra mile

You blink. Next to your name tag: an overflowing ashtray, and a half-empty packet of paracetamol. You remember reading something about paracetamol, how it doesn't just block up pain, it blocks up how you see pain. In others. Not just physical pain, like emotional suffering. You can't actually recognise it or tell what it is in the same way, under the drugs. You think: like we need to feel pain, then. To be able to understand each other, to know each other, to live together.

You'd read something similar about Facebook. How it fucks with developing brains and shit. If you're just firing words in one direction like bullets, you don't actually see the effect in person of the things you say, at some age your developing brain just skips over the empathy bit. It misses the lesson, and you don't ever get it back.

You open your eyes wider. Bright light. Sharp pain. You reach for the paracetamol. You think: probably just as fucking well. You think: too much empathy is a fucking killer. In fact empathy can gigantically go and fuck itself. Your own shit is enough shit.

You turn on the TV. It is 3.17am. The Discovery Channel is showing on old documentary about the fall of the Roman Empire. You notice a weird smell in the air. Like chlorine. Mixed with fire. The narrator tells you that all great empires reach their most aggressive at the point before they collapse. You light a spliff. Billowing white blue smoke. The heat in your veins slows to a simmer. You flick the channel. Sky News 24 tells you that France is still in an extended state of emergency. The naked words land like an anvil in your exhausted brain. Extended state of emergency. Wow. Those are exactly the perfect words to describe like just your normal now.

*

You sit in the leather chair in your office on Floor 22. Your desk spread out before you, the city stretching out behind you and beneath you as you work, work, work, work, work.

Working endlessly without pause through the cadences and rhythms of the data, the city flickers like computer graphics pulsing like a heart from day to night to day again. You feel your body wilt, your mind swirl and slow, hypnotic, you need to stop. Your body knows you need to stop, but you push on. You tell yourself: Mercy, come on. You deal in Futures. There are opportunities here, come on.

The sky outside glows a little brighter. You feel a tiny buzzing in your ears, a constant electrical hum. The kind of sound that should be too high to hear but somehow isn't. Distant, yet everywhere. Like it's coming from beyond the glass of the windows, from the sky, from the city itself.

You push on. You've been watching a pattern these last twelve hours. Something you've never seen before. Tiny, almost imperceptible irregularities in the markets. Responding to – something. On the horizon. Feverish, pulling on you like gravity –

Something aligns. Like the flash of light before a solar eclipse. And you see it.

You think: no.

You think: it can't be.

You think: but it is. Of course. Of course it is.

Not a crash. Not like that. Bigger.

Ashen earth on your tongue. A ringing in your ears. The smell of chlorine and burning. You look up.

Something fundamental. Something that means we can't just carry on. Something big. It's coming. It's coming now.

*

You. You sit outside an upmarket café in the centre of town. You wipe red lipstick from the side of your white cup. You don't like leaving marks. You ask your friend if she can hear a weird ringing sound in her ears. Your friend sips on her flat white and shakes her head.

*

You. You wait at a bus stop on the edge of town. You know the bus can be anything up to fifteen minutes late and you will still make it to the Job Centre interview on time. You look at your phone. The bus is twenty minutes late. You re-read the bus stop advert trying not to think of the consequences. The advert is trying to sell you an expensive watch. You know there is a cruel joke in this somewhere but you can't pin down exactly what it is.

*

You. You stand on a train flicking through the pages of the unwieldy broadsheet newspaper that you hate but buy anyway. More blah about Europe. Some pictures of foreigners. Something about a famous person who has died, another one. Something about Syria. Something about something else. The man next to you smells of cheese and onion crisps and you wanna get off.

*

You. You prepare a political speech written by someone else about a thing that you don't believe in at all. The news cameras roll. Your hands sweat.

*

You. You stare blankly at Instagram because you forgot to include it on the blocked sites app that was supposed to help your mind focus. That pop star Léon has posted seventeen pictures of bees and you don't know why.

*

You. You sit on the couch texting your wife who sits at the opposite end of the living room in silence. It's easier than talking sometimes. On the TV you see images of ancient city ruins buried under the earth in Cambodia. Pictures of temples under centuries old tree roots.

*

You. You sit in the toilet cubicle. You sit. Your mouth tastes of dirt and dry and smoke and bleurgh. You've been hiding, behind the bike shed, smoking. And now here.

In front of you, there is a door. On the door, there is writing.
Graffiti. Some of it is scratched in with a coin, some of it is written
in biro or marker. It has like phone numbers and jokes and a kind
of running commentary on what boys are hot and a probably racist
cartoon drawing of Miss Neil giving Mr Ahmed a handjob. And
over all of it, a fresh one in thick black letters reads: ASH IS A
SLAG.

The toilet lights are those ones that only come on when you walk
under them. They'd switched off ages ago. They didn't know you
were there. Invisible. Good. The only light is the pale white light
forcing its way in through the window, like an unwelcome guest,
like an attacker.

In the far corner of the room there is a loudspeaker, a tannoy
system. It's playing Mr Ahmed's voice, speaking to the school
assembly. An assembly has been called, an emergency assembly.

You told your mum this would happen. You told her to just shut up
about it.

Matthew had stayed off sick today. Coward Cunt.

You listen to Mr Ahmed talking about sexting and cyberbullying
and other words that nobody actually uses, like ever. He's talking
about an image. He doesn't say your name. But everyone knows,
they've all seen it. An unacceptable image.

You sit, head in your hands, thinking of everyone sat there. Silent.
Trying not to laugh. Trying to make each other laugh.

You feel the walls closing in. You take your fist and scrunch it into
a little ball, as tight as you can manage, and push it deep into your
mouth. You feel spit dribble down your wrist. You clench your
eyes tight shut. You hear a high-pitched ringing in your ears,
mixing with the noise from the tannoy system which fills your
head. You feel the hard skin of your knuckles under your teeth. You
bite down into the skin. You tear at it. You draw blood. It runs thick
and dark and red through your fingers.

Face scrunched up, eyes clenched tight shut, spit and blood
running down your arm you let out the deepest darkest harshest

silent scream and you just want to fucking die, for everyone to just fucking. Die.

*

You knock back another vodka and spill half of it across your suit trousers but you don't notice. Dirty electro and RnB beats fill the air of this half-empty room. The woman stood in front of you still dances. You drink another vodka.

You tell her: I think something big might be happening. Is. Is happening.

She dances. You drink. You throw some bank notes down. You tell her: My name's Mercy, what's yours?

She dances. You tell her: This isn't the kind of place I'd normally come to. My colleagues – that's how I know. I needed to speak to someone about – tried calling my dad. Voicemail woman. There wasn't anyone.

I've been busy. I've been too busy you see for you know. Friends and things.

She dances. You drink. You say: What's your name? Please? Is it Ruby? Is that your real name, Ruby? I'm telling you we can't just carry on Ruby. They are though. All of them. They said, you're talking about an opportunity right? I said no, fucking no, not this time! They told me to go home, lie down. Said I was being irrational, emotional – aggressive Ruby! Security came, took my fob key, chucked me out like this fucking –

You drink. She dances. You say: I am someone who reads the signs. You see? I deal in Futures, it's what I do. You see all this, Ruby? This suit. This money I'm throwing at your feet. This distance between us. It only means anything because we say it does. Because of a future we say exists. But it does not exist. It does not. Because I have seen it. The end. It is coming. I have seen it.

She dances. You say: I didn't want to know this, I didn't ask for this. I didn't, I did not. She dances. You talk. She dances. You drink. She dances. You pay. She dances. You leave.

Staggering, heavy night air enveloping your hammered face you make your way down a filthy bin alley and blink, to focus, to see as you squat and piss. It runs in angular streams through the cobbles, lapping at the heels of your shoes. You slump onto your arse, head in your hands. You feel a noise rising up through you, like choking on tears, only not tears just empty abandoned convulsing nothing in your exhausted no-sleep body as your vision blacks out like a broken screen, Mercy. Eyes wide open, mind still racing you see nothing but black, hear nothing but the chokes of your own voice.

I'm not wrong. You say out loud, into the darkness. About these things, I'm not.

The dark nothing pulses red and purple and orange. You feel your body throw out a hand as your face collides with the wet cobblestones.

You are better than this, you think. You are someone who reads the signs. You are a sign reader. A future teller. A soothsayer.

Mercy, you are a prophet.

Your vision returns in blurs. You say it aloud.

I am a prophet.

And you know. You know. You know that now it is time to act.

*

You will admit when you make mistakes
You will express ideas concisely
You will communicate with conviction
You will communicate sensitively
You will paint a clear picture
You will not agree blandly with others
You will listen
You will be happy and sincere

You call out the coffee order. Price the sandwich, the drink, and popcorn snack. Smile. Take the money. Give the change. Almost yawn. Don't yawn. Smile.

The customer says: thanks Abdullah. Fuck did he know your name, is that some kind of racist shit, some kind of guess? Your name tag. Of course, your name tag. You call out the coffee order.

On the way in passing the billboards, the adverts, the KEEP CALM AND CARRY ON poster, you'd felt like this burning sensation through your whole body, a white light behind your eyes, this hot tingling all over your skin. You'd blazed a joint to settle things.

You feel the manager watching you: be people-perfect. Smile. High five. Go team.

You were going to need another smoke soon, or you were going to fucking kill her. Someone here was going to fucking die.

You give the change. You smile. You say thanks. Your hand trembles. You hear noise outside. People singing. Or shouting. You look through the glass doors, the glass shop front, to see: A man with a beard. Wearing only his pants. He is grinning. And hopping from foot to foot. Another man. Also with a beard. Also in his pants. He is carrying a djembe. And a woman. A white woman with dreadlocks and a glittery bikini waving around a homemade flag that says: BANKS ARE WANKS. You look back to the customer. You strain to smile.

They come in. They come in to the store. You think: oh fuck.

They sing:

Hey everybody! Put your shopping down!

Hey everybody! Put the credit cards down!

No more shopping! Try buying nothing!

The answer is inside you and the answer is love!

Everyone watches. The drummer in his pants dances up to the till. You think: oh fuck.

You think: undercover monitoring? Mystery shoppers. This is exactly the kind of dick move the district manager would pull.

Your manager is stood right next to you. She's watching you. The pants guy is right up in your face.

You think: Be warm. Be open. Good service means turning nobody away, means meeting the customer on their terms, being malleable to their needs.

Put down your money! Search deep inside!

Hey, hug your neighbour!

People of the high street, let's make a new high street!

Come on, come on, throw away your money and dance!

The drummer is going wild. The girl is waving her flag around: BANKS ARE WANKS. People have come in from the street to watch, they're watching you. The pants guy dances towards you, your manager is staring you down –

You think: fucking bastards trying to catch me out.

You think: she's watching.

You think: I need this job.

You think: be people-perfect. Don't fuck up. Pass. This. Test!

*

Fuck, fuck, fuck the fucking world and literally fuck everything. Why must this shit always happen to you?

The cocaine circulates through your bloodstream. You push on the accelerator. You race at sixty through the inner city.

Get out of my way fuckers, I've got too much to do, I don't have time for this shit!

You tell the guy next you: Why do these people never understand, Jeff? I've got a fucking campaign to announce, Jeff. About fucking bees! Jeff says, I think you can slow down a bit.

And now my girlfriend is at the hospital, Jeff, a proper hospital with babies and everything, and she *needs me* and I can't even be there because there's too much to do, and do the shitheads understand how that *feels*? Do they? No!

Jeff is silent.

There's only one review I kept, Jeff. Not many people know that. I'm telling you a secret about me, Jeff, a secret. It's important.

Jeff nods.

The only one I kept. Everyone else said I was stealing. A plagiarist. It was sampling, Jeff. Sampling. Like in hip hop. Yeah?

Jeff nods. Watch out!

But one – this one – she said, I know it exactly, Jeff, she said, 'This album is a search for meaning. It's what pop music *needs now*. Assembled in patchwork style, Léon sifts through the debris of a collapsing world, sorting through the driftwood in attempt to make sense of the wreckage. With booty- shaking beats.' Isn't that beautiful? Jeff? Jeff? Jeff. Jeff? Jeff.

Jeff nods.

I'm just a man, Jeff. Just a man, trying to do something real! Trying to make a difference.

You clench your teeth. A rush of blood to the head. You smell rubber as you screech around the corner.

Tell me a secret about you, Jeff! I told you a secret about me. I want to know a secret about you. Jeff!

Jeff looks at this phone, as your Porsche careers around another bend. He says. Um. It's the publicist. He wants to know exactly what it is you plan to do about the bees.

Do your eyes hurt, Jeff? My eyes hurt. Is the light weird?

A dog runs in front of the car! You pull a hard right to swerve out of the way! The world outside the car spins and spins and spins in a blur as your world inside the car and inside your mind slows to nothing. Jeff screams, but you hear nothing. All you see as your body is pulled forwards like a whip is: Your childhood driveway.

Your mother calling. Amy backstage, when you met her. Yourself,
onstage alone so far from the crowd, so far, alone as the car spins,
and the world floods back in, Jeff's screams filling your ears. And –

*

You step into the station. The station full of people. You watch the
people walking without looking at each other. The way they
navigate the space between each other without looking at each
other. You watch the people walking looking straight ahead. The
people walking looking at their feet. The people walking looking at
the timetables. The people walking looking at the billboards. The
people walking looking at their phones.

You are a prophet. You have come with a message. Mercy, you
come with a truth.

Ahead of you, there is a sign. You recognise the sign. You recognise
it from everywhere like a mantra in different shapes, different
varieties in this carnival of denial we are dancing this dance in.
White text against a red backdrop: KEEP CALM AND CARRY ON.

You think: no.

You approach the sign. People walking past you. You dig your
hands into the plastered paper of the sign. You feel it under your
fingernails, like chalk, like wood. You clench your fingers. You tear
the sign. You tear it down. You tear it down. You tear it down.

You clutch the tatters of the shredded sign. You raise your head,
you open your chest. You walk in to the centre of the concourse.
You throw the ragged sign to the ground! You declare to the
people: I am someone who reads signs. I have a message. I am a
message!

The people walk past you. You feel yourself rise as you declare: I
deal in Futures! And I have seen it! That the end of this world is
coming!

The people look past you and look through you. The way they look
through drunk people, through mad people, through old people.
Unwilling to see you, incapable of seeing you. You rise, ten feet

tall, towering as you declare: we have built this world this now in the service of a future that does not exist, that never did exist.

They walk past you. You Mercy, twenty, fifty, one hundred feet tall, fire in your eyes in your breath, proclaiming: Lift up your heads, and see! We have created this world, this world that destroys us! That will destroy us!

They walk past you. One thousand feet tall, towering over the city, they walk past you. Towering up, up, up the city streets revealing themselves to you like lines in the palm of your hand, they walk past you!

You declare to the city: look! Look around you! We have created this world, there is more than this world, we are more than this world that will end! Look and see that I am here! I am here! I am here!

And you are here! You are what is here! You are the stuff that is here, that lives here. Towering high above the city, you are the city!

You are re-development and planning process and new investment and corporate interest. You are gentrification and demolition and forgotten past. You are residential zones, commercial zones, casino, police station, mayor's house, school.

You are libraries and drop-in-centres and hospitals. You are buildings which used to be libraries, drop-in centres, and hospitals.

You are a district full of students, you are a district full of suits, you are a district full of hipsters. You are a district full of aspirational middle class families with two kids, you are a district full of working class families with no work. You are the district where the Eastern Europeans live which used to be where the Pakistanis live which used to be where the Irish live which used to be where the Jewish live.

You are housing schemes with pretty names which no buses go to any more. You are absurd civic corridors. You are vomit on the corner. You are gum on the bus seats, you are CCTV, you are the graffiti wall of the underground pedestrian tunnel.

And you are the weather, the sun, the moon and the air. You are all the lives that live and that lived. You are all the loves that love and were loved. You are high street coffee outlets. You are dust particles. You are breath.

And you are Ash, alone in the toilet cubicle as your uncertain body is turned into a dumping ground for the anxieties of boys, tasting blood on your tongue like copper, like coins.

And you are Léon, lost, gasping into the wheel of a freshly crashed Porsche, a brand, a self-perpetuating idea of an idea of a person, addicted to being needed, to being seen, to feeling loved with no real sense at all of what that even fucking means.

And you are Abdullah, trapped behind the counter, monitored, surveyed, projecting a self for someone else, wearing a smile that barely conceals a torrent of blood in you that boils.

And you are Mercy, one thousand feet tall, invisible, declaring that we are more than this story we've told ourselves and that what is true now has always been true: that any future we ever did have or may have begins and ends in what we have here, in what we have now, in what we do here, in what we do now. You Mercy, fifty, twenty, five feet tall, demanding: lift up your heads. And see. That I am here and you are here and what we have is now.

And you are a man, sat at a desk, telling a story about the end of the world. And you are sat in a room in this city, listening to a man tell a story which he has told you is about the end of the world.

And he knows that you know that it's only the end of the world in this story because he's decided that it has to be, as he speaks and says that I am here. And you are here. And what we have is now.

And you are Mercy and you are Abdullah and you are Léon and you are Ash.

And he's decided that it has to be because the weight of world that you live in is killing you, because your bodies and hearts cannot carry it. And he's decided that it has to be because it's easier to imagine the end of this world than it is to imagine what a new one might look like. And he's decided that is has to be because he wants you, each of you Mercy, Abdullah, Léon, Ash, to face up to something that you all deeply know, and Mercy you know for sure. What each of you feels but can't speak. The light in the sky, the smell in the air, the hum in the background, unspoken. To be made at this point in the story, unavoidable. As each head in the city lifts up, looks out the window, looks to the sky to see: the truth you already knew. That this world cannot continue. That this will not continue. That this has to stop. This has to stop. This has to stop.

And everyone in this city can see that it is going to. Now.

A crashing noise. It is the sound of all of the lives of this city at breaking point. **Kieran** *sits in this noise, in sweat, hurt, and exhaustion. Eventually, he fades the noise out, giving way to choral ethereal music.*

*

The bearded man in the pants is still here. The djembe guy is still here. The white woman with the dreadlocks and the glittery bikini, she's still here. People have started walking out of the shop. Into the street. Covering their ears from the deafening sub-sonic hum, looking up to the sky that begins to burn now bright and white. Someone screams. You blink. Your name tag still says: Abdullah. You. You, for now, are still here.

*

You came, he says to you. Matthew. He looks you in the eye, he says: Ash. Ash, you came.

You tell him: don't get fucking smug about it, alright?

Is it true, he asks. Is it really happening?

You tell him: seems to be.

*

You stand alone by the wreckage of your fucked car. Jeff abandoned you like everyone else, the bastard, running off in some kind of deranged fit. Not this, he said. Not with you Léon you twat, not this.

You look out over the streets now bathed in light, filled with people, the roads littered with cars at a standstill. You think: she needs me.

Eyes throbbing, chemicals coursing through your veins, you charge your way on foot. To the hospital.

*

The customer in front of you – is he still a customer? Now? The *man* in front of you tries to buy a coffee. He just wants to buy a coffee, like he doesn't know what else to do, like he just wants to carry on.

You tell him: get it your fucking self.

It just comes out, like it makes sense to say it. You don't smile. You don't need to smile, not now. And the customer – not customer man – stops still, and in what seems like slow motion leaps over the counter and starts grabbing things, stuffing his pockets! Your manager has run out into the streets joining the crowds outside. Other people join in with the looting, filling their pockets and bags full of little muffins wrapped in cellophane, panini sandwiches, biscotti. And something rises inside of you – inside of you, Abdullah and it's like, this sound like laughter only it's not laughter, it's just air escaping from your lungs as the looters turn the guts of this place inside out!

*

Matthew just stands there. He says nothing. There is nothing to say. You think, for a brief tiny moment that saying nothing, now, in response to this, is the most perfect thing he's ever done, the fucking bastard.

Then he says, eyes wide in something like fear: what? Really, actually happening? Like in films and that?

You fucking dickhead, Matthew, you say. You have to fucking ruin everything don't you?

What? He says, eyes welling up begging now. It's not my fault this is happening! Is it? Is it?

He looks at you. And you look at him.

You say: take off your shirt.

He stands, lost.

Just fucking do it, Matthew.

*

You bulldoze your way through the hospital corridors. Amy I'm coming! AMY!

You follow the signs. Maternity ward. You shout. AMY! You push open each door. Confused, terrified women stare back at you. And then, she's there. In bed. Skin damp, face red, hair matted.

You swallow. And you speak. Amy, you say. I'm here. I'm here.

*

The man in his pants looks at you. You hold his gaze. The fucking sneaky undercover mystery shopper dressed up bastard boss cunt. He's still looking at you. You think, you don't *need* this, you don't *need* this, not now.

You shout: fucking sack me now hey you fucking nasty piece of spying shit!

He looks back at you. He says: um, sorry what?

You tear off your name tag: Abdullah. You throw it to the floor. Fucking nice try pal! You jump over the counter and grab his naked beardy skinny fuck body and throw *him* to the floor. Everyone that wasn't screaming already is screaming now as you pound his stupid cunt face with your fists like mincemeat, blood spilling from his mouth and crack – your jaw shudders as white dreadlock girl's boot swipes across your face and the man in his pants with the pounded bloody beard is on top of *you* now knocking shit out of *you* now, crashes of searing hot pain and it feels kind of brilliant! Kind of brilliant and real!

*

Matthew pulls off his t-shirt. He doesn't know what else to do. He is glad, probably, of the guidance.

New downy gingery hair trembles on his breastplate. On his arms, blue veins push against his pale white skin. The inside of him. What's inside of him. Like lines on a map. A streetmap of the city.

I fucking hate you for what you did, Matthew, do you understand that?

He nods.

Good, you say. Good.

Now do you remember Miss Neil's lesson about Pompeii?

He shakes his head.

You do, Matthew! You do, you say. About the volcano. When everything got wiped out. And the people were frozen in ash. My name! Like statues. Remember?

He blubs. He nods.

Like, that's all that carried on. Into the next thing. That moment frozen in ash.

Snot runs into Matthew's whimpering mouth. But there's not, there's . . .

What? Speak up. Speak up, Matthew, I can't understand you!

But there's not a next thing! He says. After this, there's not!

You look at him. You say: Matthew. There's always a next thing. You just haven't thought about what it might be yet.

You say: Matthew look at me.

He looks at you.

You say: hold my hand.

He looks at you.

You say: hold my fucking hand you cunt.

He reaches out his hand.

*

I'm here. I'm here, you say. I told Jeff the bees would have to fucking wait, that I had to get *here*. He fucked off. I walked. Amy!

And then you see. Swaddled up at Amy's breast. A tiny head.

You ask: Is that? Is that, the, your. Our. Is that it, that's what it is, that's it there?

Amy nods. You stand still. She says: She's sleeping. Would you like to. . .? She gestures to join. You stagger towards the bed. Legs like jelly. And you kneel.

You say: you. . . you didn't need me.

And Amy takes your hand and places it on top of the child's head. It is warm and soft like nothing on earth. And you forget to breathe.

And Amy looks you in the eye and she says: no. No we didn't need you. No we did not.

*

Hot shocks of pain rushing through your flesh, your face, your head, your bones, your very bones Abdullah, as the two of you roll on top of and through each other becoming one thing, one panting sweating, ugly red bleeding broken flesh of a one thing. The shells that you wear burst open, smashed open to the world until neither of you can take anymore and you stop.

Gasping for breath. Your back on the cold floor. His face held above yours. The smell of him, like meat. And you hold each other's gaze. You feel him see you. Feel you here. You're here.

And you see him. And you see: he's not a fucking undercover mystery shopper. He's just some daft protestor hippy prick. And you think: oh mate. And you hold onto his bloody sodden hair. And he looks at you. And he holds you. And you're about to speak, to say: something. And he opens his mouth. And you yours. And then. Just at that minute –

An audible in-breath.

*

And a tiny eyelid opens. And another one. You do not breathe. And all the anxieties of ever and right now just fall away. Not even euphoric or anything. So much more just normal. Like you can feel inside your bones how you've known each other forever. And of course, in her case, that's literally actually true.

And the light outside the window glows stronger, drenching this room in bright white light, like in soft focus. And it can't be the end of the world anymore because you sit there holding her in silence for what must actually be forever.

Short sharp sobs bubble to the surface of your body, beyond your control, becoming a cascade of crying and wailing and shaking. And Amy puts her arm around you, and you sink completely into her. You remember to breathe. And everything makes a kind of sense, if only in this moment.

I'm here, you say. You just say, I'm here. I'm here. I'm here.

And then –

An audible in-breath.

*

You open the window, and climb out. Matthew follows. Your small bodies fit on the windowsill, perched, legs dangling above the street below. People filling the roads. Light filling the sky. You look up at the sky. Burning silver yellow red and white and fierce and hot.

You light a cigarette. You say to Matthew: twos? It's my last one.

Some people below fall to their knees. Some people take out their phones.

Apocalypse selfies.

A bee buzzes past you. Matthew flinches. Chill out, you say. They only sting when they're panicking. Breathe.

Matthew squeezes your hand tight. The bee lands on his naked arm. It crawls along his skin. Then flies off.

You feel Matthew's sweat mix with yours in your palm. Without looking at you, between little gasps he says: You know at the end of *Final Fantasy VII*, how it's the end of the world and maybe it's a good thing? Like, maybe this'll be like that?

And you want to say: fucking hell Matthew you always have to fucking ruin everything don't you! And you want to say: yeah. That's it. That's it exactly. And you haven't decided which.

A tiny clump of ash falls from your cigarette, into the dust of the city air. And then, just at that moment –

An audible in-breath.

*

You stumble into the park. You are exhausted. You are dizzy. You are dazed.

The people gather. Gathering in crowds, the way they gather to watch the scheduled demolition of a tower block. Gathering to see it all come crashing down. The end of things.

I told you, you think. I fucking told you.

You sit on the park bench. Still. Invisible. And you notice yourself breathe. In your pocket you feel something. A fountain pen. Gold. From a desk. A desk you used to sit at once.

All around you people are running or screaming or dancing or singing or hugging or crying or praying or none, none of these things.

You tried to tell them. You tried. Not to turn it around. Just to give them a moment. To see what they know. That this world we've created will end. Just to give everyone a bit of a heads up.

You take off your shoes and your stockings. Methodically, you roll up your stocking into balls and place them inside your shoes. You place the pen from your pocket next to the shoes. Tidy. Neat.

Pleasing.

You feel the grass beneath your feet. Cold and tickly. You feel the earth, the very earth, between your toes.

You reach down to your left, and pluck a flower from the earth. A yellow tulip. You smell the tulip. It smells faint. But fresh. And clean.

Someone runs towards you, and past you, screaming. Trying to run, trying to run from the sky. You stay still. You breathe in deep. And gently close your eyes.

You feel the warmth from the sky upon your face.

You feel the air against your cheek.

You feel the earth beneath your feet.

You are here. You are the stuff that is here.

You are this air that was always just air.

You are this sky that was always just sky.

You are this earth and this land that was always just land and recognised nothing that was ever built on it.

At the end there was just this. This, and only this.

You smell the tulip, clean and light and soft and fresh.

And then.

That's it.

An audible in-breath. **Kieran** *blows out the candle. End.*

Mouthpiece

Kieran Hurley

Mouthpiece by Kieran Hurley, commissioned by the Traverse Theatre was first performed at the Traverse Theatre, Scotland, on 5 December 2018 with the following cast:

Declan   Lorn Macdonald
Libby   Neve McIntosh

Creative team

Writer: Kieran Hurley
Director: Orla O'Loughlin
Set, Lighting and Projection Designer: Kai Fischer
Composer and Sound Designer: Kim Moore
Costume Designer: Sophie Ferguson
Fight Director: Raymond Short

Production team

Production Manager: Kevin McCallum
Chief Electrician: Renny Robertson
Head of Stage: Gary Staerck
Lighting and Sound Technician: Tom Saunders
Company Stage Manager: Gemma Turner
Deputy Stage Manager: Gillian Richards
Stage Management Work Placement: Bekah Astles

It returned to the Traverse Theatre, Scotland in August 2019 for the Edinburgh Festival Fringe before touring internationally with the following cast:

Libby   Shauna Macdonald
Declan   Angus Taylor

The Associate Director was Katherine Nesbitt.

Mouthpiece transferred to the Soho Theatre, London and was first performed on 1 April 2019. It returned to the Traverse Theatre, Scotland in August 2019 for the Edinburgh Festival Fringe.

Scene One

Projected text appears somewhere on stage in a serif typeface like Courier or Times. It reads: MOUTHPIECE.

Libby   The opening image. This is the beginning of the story, and it's vital. It should ideally set up the place, the world of it all. And it's good if we can meet the characters already in the middle of something high stakes. A sense of a story already in motion. It should establish the theme and the tone, and give us a snapshot of the characters' struggles.

Some things are just rules. There are rules to make things work and this is no different, really.

Scene Two

Projected text, as before. It reads: Salisbury Crags, Edinburgh. Twilight.

It reads: A woman.

Libby *stands at the edge, looking down. She swigs from a hip flask.*

Projected text reads: A boy.

Some way off, **Declan** *sits with a pad and pencil, looking out.*

Libby   I dunno how quickly a body falls. The Crags are less high than they look, probably. I mean they feel high – oh Jesus – they do feel high. But that's 'cause it's the only bit up here that's like a proper sheer drop. Straight down. I'd give it two, maybe three seconds. Two and a half, maybe. One elephant, two elephant, three ele – splat.

She drinks.

Town's beginning to light up. Twinkly. Like in a story book. Or like the jewelry box of your lonely aging mother. All shiny and presentable and completely coldly fucking indifferent.

Declan *starts packing all his stuff up into a plastic bag.*

Does it feel sore? When you land? Or do you just not even know? You'd probably have to feel something, it's not like you get to just click an off switch. At least a moment of pain, like a sudden burst. But so intense that you don't even recognise it as pain at all, like when you accidentally grab something burning hot and for the briefest second it feels ice cold. A flash of that. And then – gone. The pain is gone. I mean that's the point right?

She takes a step closer to the edge. She opens out her arms.

One elephant, two elephant, three –

She closes her eyes. **Declan** *sees her. She lifts her leg.*

Declan *grabs* **Libby**.

Libby   Jesusfuck!

She starts to hit **Declan**.

You, you – get, just you get – get off me! Get the fuck away from me!

Declan *holds* **Libby**.

Declan   Breathe, just breathe, you're okay!

Libby   Fuck you!

Declan   Right. Right. Gies your phone I'm gonnae call an ambulance –

Libby   I don't need a fucking ambulance.

Declan   Samaritans then. Talk sense intae you.

Libby   I – I slipped. I just slipped. You scared me and I – I slipped.

Declan   Did you fuck.

Libby   You shouldn't be fucking creeping up on people. Okay? Idiot!

Declan   Eh? Fuck were you playing at standing up at the edge like that then?

Beat.

Libby   Tai Chi.

Declan   What?

Libby   I was doing Tai Chi.

Declan   Aye very good.

Libby *fumbles for her hip flask.*

Declan   You been drinking?

Declan *grabs the flask and sniffs it.*

Fucksake!

Libby *snatches the flask back.*

Libby   That's none of your business!

Declan   Fine. Fucking fine then. You ken it's actually very fucking selfish hen, you ken that? Have you no got folk who – cunts who need you? Look, fuck – they'll be able to say it better, the Samaritans. Fucksake! You no got kids to hink aboot or that, nut?

She takes a drink.

Declan   Right, fine then. Whatever. I'm in a fucking rush eh. And Gary'll actual kill me, so –

Declan *starts gathering up his stuff.* **Libby** *picks up one of* **Declan***'s drawings.*

Libby   Is this – you did this?

Declan   Fucksake! Bus pass. Fucking buss pass man! Here have you seen – have you seen like a wee bus pass? Wi like a picture ay like this face on it?

Declan *points to his own face.* **Libby** *glances around, shakes her head.*

Aw naw man! Right I need to run. Or I am actually dead.

Libby   Where is it you're rushing to?

Declan   There.

Libby   Where?

Declan   See they flats?

Libby   You're running all the way there?

Declan   Well, looks like it now does it no?

Libby *chuckles, amazed.* **Declan** *waits, expectant, hand outstretched.* **Libby** *realises:*

Libby   Oh! I'm so sorry I don't have any change, for your bus, I can't –

Declan   Naw hen. You've still got ma drawing.

Libby   Ah! Right.

Beat.

I like it.

Declan   Right. Keep that one then. If you want.

Libby   Really?

Declan   It's shite, have it. But dae me a favour right, this bit round here's my private bit. And I really need it right. So gonnae like fucking keep away –

Libby   What did you say your name was again?

Declan   Declan Swan.

Libby   Declan.

Declan   Aye.

Libby   I'm Libby. Hi.

Declan   Look, sorry right but I really do need tae fuckin bolt.

Scene Three

Projected text reads: Libby. At home.

Libby   Mum doesn't hear me come in. Good. She's in the kitchen, dotting about sozzled, Radio Four blasting through the walls. Creep upstairs, into the bathroom and chuck water over my face, my eyes. All feels weirdly heightened, sharpened. Like water, but more so. Strain my neck and drink it cool from the tap, letting it pour down my chin in big grateful icy glugs. Slump down onto the hard, wet floor. And breathe.

I take that boy's drawing out my pocket. A scribbled Edinburgh skyline. And in the foreground – all detailed, and carefully wrought – a picture of a little girl. Reaching up on her tip-toes for something. Or someone. Reaching out to them. To hold their hand, maybe?

In the distance he's drawn this, like – it looks like maybe it's a sunrise. Or a moon. But actually it's a mouth. A giant blood red mouth, rising up behind the city. Open like it's saying something, or like it's about to eat everything up. Consume it. I stick it up there, next to the mirror, and I stare at it. All dark and fierce and sort of blissfully naively sincere. Like something I might have done, when I was his age. It pierces the blank white walls like a fresh tattoo. I love it.

I find a pen, and I search for a scrap of paper; an old bus ticket. Sitting there on the bathroom floor I write; *A boy. On top of a hill, looking out over the city.* I write: *looking out and drawing.* I write: *falling, running, and a picture of a little girl.*

Scene Four

Projected text reads: Salisbury Crags. *It reads:* A boy.

Declan *sits, with a pencil and a pad in front of him. His face is bruised. He clenches his fists. He stares at his paper. He starts to draw.*

Libby *approaches.*

Libby   Hi. Hello. Hi.

Declan *looks at* **Libby**. *He looks away again. He continues to draw.*

Thought I'd find you here. Eventually.

Beat.

Libby   I'm not – I'm not interrupting am I?

Declan   Aye. Actually. As it happens.

Libby   Your drawing –

Declan   Yes. Yes I am drawing. The now. So –

Libby   No, I mean your drawing. You gave me. I just wanted to say –

Libby *sees* **Declan**'*s bruises.*

Bloody hell what happened to your face?

Declan *turns away. He draws.*

Was it Gary?

Declan   How do you ken aboot Gary?

Libby   You told me. You said if you were late then Gary would –

Declan   Listen hen. Maybe I wisnae clear, sorry. But it'd be dead good if you would be so kind as to get yersel tae fuck. I come here to be alone.

Libby   Me too.

Declan   And yet somehow here we both are. If only there was some kind ay solution tae this, eh?

Libby   I just wanted to say, I like it. And maybe – would you sign it?

Declan   Taking the piss like?

Libby   No.

Declan   Look I'm really sorry about before alright, if I – I caused you any bother I apologise, right –

Libby   I just – wanted to find you. To say thank you.

Declan *continues to draw, more furiously.*

For the picture.

Declan   Look it's no like I dae proper drawings or that. Right? It's just whatever's in ma heid. I dinnae show anycunt. Wee Siân, sometimes, maybe. But that's it. Naebody kens. Nae danger. So –

Libby   I do. I've seen them.

Beat.

Declan   Look, if I sign your bit ay paper will you please beat it?

Libby   Sure.

Declan   Here.

Libby   The wee girl. In the picture. Is that your sister?

Declan   Mibbe.

Libby   What did you say her name was again, Shan?

Declan   Aye, Siân. S – i – a – n, and the *a* has a wee hingmy above it. Siân.

Libby   Siân. It's pretty.

Declan   No 'Shan' but. It's no 'shan.' Even though it sounds the same.

Libby   It's a pretty name.

Declan   Cos shan, right, is word that normally means just very shady. Or like a wee shame. Or like just like really really bad, like brutal eh, like 'that is fucking shan as fuck.'

Libby   Yeah, okay. I know.

Declan   Aye that's no what her name means but.

Libby   What does it mean?

Declan   It means God's gracious gift. Here.

Declan *hands her the picture, now signed.*

Libby   Thanks. Never know, it could be worth something now.

Declan   Aye only once I'm deid but. That's the rule is it no? And we both ken this is a nice wee secluded spot but dinnae be getting any smart ideas, alright?

Libby *smiles. Beat.*

Libby   It looks like she's reaching up for a hand, for help. Siân. The girl in your picture, I mean. Like she's scared. But looking at her, you see actually she's not. She's not the one whose scared. The picture's sad and angry, but she's not. And actually maybe it's the other way around and she's the one who is reaching up to help you –

Beat.

Um – I hope this isn't weird. Can I give you this? I got you this.

Libby *hands* **Declan** *a small box, with a ribbon around it.* **Declan** *tentatively takes it.*

Declan   Fuck's this?

Libby   Open it.

Declan *looks at the box. He opens it. It is a set of quality pencils. He looks at* **Libby**.

Declan   You got these for me?

Libby *nods.*

Declan   What for?

Libby   Um – look, I left my phone number in that box –

Declan   Phone number?

Libby   Yes. No, no not like – it's, it's just the landline. Just, if you wanted to – like meet up. And talk. About art. Art and stuff. It'd be nice to – I'd like to – I dunno.

Beat.

Libby   That didn't sound so completely weird in my head I'm sorry please don't think I'm mental.

Declan   Already signed your picture did I no?

Libby   Yes.

Declan   Well please fuck off then.

Libby   Okay. Right. Sorry. Thanks.

Libby *leaves.*

Scene Five

Declan *in his room, alone. He opens the box of pencils.*

Libby   After the set-up comes the moment where your character must make a decision to do something that changes their reality.

Declan *stares at the pencils.*

This moment is sometimes called the 'break into two' after the moment we break into act two in a traditional three act structure.

Declan *puts his hands down his pants. He holds his cock.*

But it doesn't matter if you're dealing in three acts or one, the point is your character makes a decision.

Declan *picks* **Libby***'s phone number up out of the pencil box.*

And that decision turns their familiar world upside down, or propels them out of it altogether. And sets them off on an unpredictable relationship, or an increasingly dangerous journey into the unknown.

Declan *stares at the number.*

That's the idea anyway.

Scene Six

Projected text: A café. Edinburgh New Town. Day.

Libby *has a coffee.* **Declan** *sips from a can, self-aware, on edge.*

Libby   You sure you just want a Coke?

Declan   Aye.

Libby   It's just it's like, 9.30 in the morning.

Declan   I dinnae like hot drinks.

Libby   Oh right.

Declan   Feels wrong. Feels weird. I dinnae like it.

Libby   Here, look, choose something to eat. Have whatever, it's on me.

Declan   What is it you wanted tae talk aboot?

Libby   Well I'd like to talk about you, your art – if you're up for it.

Declan   How like?

Libby   I've got some ideas for maybe some places and galleries and things I could show you. If you like. But only if –

Declan   Naw, I meant like how as in why.

Libby   Oh. Right.

Declan   'Art is anal produce.'

Libby   Sorry?

Declan   'Art is anal produce.' That's what it says. Here, what the fuck is this place?

Libby   Oh, um – *artisanal*. Um. *Artisanal* produce, it just means – it means like it's all good stuff.

Declan   Right.

Beat.

Libby   Have you ever been to the National Gallery of Modern Art?

Declan *shakes his head.*

Libby   I thought we could have a look there if you want.

Declan   Am I allowed?

Libby   Well, yes it's, it's a public gallery everyone's allowed –

Declan   Is there no like a dress code or that. They'll let me in?

Libby   Yes – ha, of course they will, Declan – there's an exhibition on that I think you'd maybe like. Or there's the Portrait Gallery, or the National Gallery. Or –

Declan *is staring at the menu, overwhelmed.*

Libby   Honestly choose whatever you like.

Declan   Can I just have like a bacon roll or that?

Libby   Yeah, I'm sure they could do that. You know what, I'm going to have that too. I might have a bit of avocado on mine, do you want some?

Declan   What on like a breakfast roll? On like meat?

Libby   Yes.

Declan   That is wrong as fuck by the way. You're a wrong yin.

Libby   Right, well –

Declan   Wrong.

Libby   Okay. Okay.

Long pause.

Libby   So there's the Gallery of Modern Art, the National Gallery, the Portrait Gallery –

Declan   Why are you doing this?

Libby   I just – I think your drawings are very, very good and, I'd like to, help. See if I can help. Until you're ready to maybe share it with, you know – the people in your life. Gary, your mum. Your friends –

Declan   I dinnae have any friends.

Libby   Well, you know, I just think someone coming from your neighbourhood, your community –

Declan   My 'community'?

Libby   Yes.

Declan   Right. You're one ay they cunts. Got it.

Libby   Excuse me?

Declan   Here's one for you right, a wee joke for you, you might like this. A toilet joke, right. Boy fae Muirhoose and a boy fae Morningside in a toilet, right. Next tae each other. Pissing in the same big bit. Muirhoose cunt shakes off, zips up, heads for the door. Morningside boy goes 'Dearie me. Did your mother never teach you to wash your hands?' Muirhoose cunt turns roond, goes 'Naw, she taught me no tae piss on ma fingers.'

Beat.

Naw? Aye me neither, it's no really laugh out loud is it? But the point is: see cunts like the Muirhoose cunt, he gets on wi things, dealing wi his ain problems. As they affect him. Cunts like the Morningside cunt just want tae show every other cunt in the room how clean their fucking hands are.

Libby   Okay. I get it. I'm the Morningside cunt aren't I. In this scenario.

Declan   It doesnae mean what you think it means. Like vagina. But bad.

Libby   I'm not from Morningside.

Declan   Aye, and I'm no fae Muirhoose pal, so what's your point?

Libby   I'm just saying that I'm interested in you, your story – and that since we met –

Declan   Sorry to disappoint you right, but I dinnae have a story.

Libby   Everyone has a story.

Declan   Naw. Some ay us just have lives.

Beat.

Libby   Okay. Cool. I'm sorry, really, if I came across all 'Common People'.

Beat.

You're probably right this was silly, I didn't mean to –

Declan   What's 'Common People'?

Libby   You know, Pulp? 'She came from Greece she had a thirst for knowledge' – No?

Declan   You're weird.

Libby   Cheers.

Beat.

Declan   How's it you're so intae art and that anyway?

Libby   Sorry?

Declan   How'd you ken so much about like art and that?

Libby   Well, I suppose I'm a writer. Used to be. I used to be a writer, so –

Declan   What sort ay writing?

Libby   Hmm?

Declan   You're a writer. Used to be. What did you write?

Libby   Plays.

Declan   What do you mean plays?

Libby   Sorry?

Declan   What do you mean plays? What's plays?

Libby   What are plays?

Beat.

Declan   Aye.

Libby   I don't think anyone has ever asked me that before.

Declan   Right, well, look I'm just saying, I ken what they *are* right, but just like – like, ken, we had someone come and dae drama once. At the centre. Made us dae they Hot Seats. It's like that right, is that what it is?

Libby   Um, no not – sort of I mean, I – it's just stories really. Like on TV. But happening in the same room. In a theatre.

Declan   What's the point in that?

Libby   Ha! I, um – good question. I –

Declan   Is it wi singers?

Libby   Sorry?

Declan   You've got singers in it don't you?

Libby   No. Not in the sort of plays I do, no.

Declan   What sort of plays dae you dae like?

Libby   I don't – I don't know. Actually. Anymore.

Declan   That's why you're a writer-used-to-be aye?

Libby   It's not as simple as that.

Declan   How?

Libby   How as in how? Or how as in why?

Declan *shrugs.*

Look it's not like quitting a job where there's like some bastard manager's office or something where you can slap your hand on the desk and storm out with your head held high. Like in films. It's quieter than that. It's just – a quiet kind of nothing that sets in, by itself. I was supposed to be one of the Next Big Things, believe it or not. When I was young.

Declan   So what happened?

Libby   I went on to be a history-making success story of course.

Beat.

Declan   Is that a joke?

Libby   Not really laugh-out-loud is it? Ach. It's complicated.

Declan   You think I'm no gonnae understand like?

Pause.

Libby   They tell you this stuff, okay, when you're just starting out. And they think they might have found the sexy new voice they've been looking for. They tell you how they love the *urgency* of what you're saying. So you leave these conversations all puffed up with the sense of your own ability and you give them what you think they've asked for.

Beat.

You give them yourself. In all its messy, painful difficulty. Okay? And they say 'um, okay, sure, but can it be a bit more like this thing which won some awards last year' or 'I just don't think our audience will buy into this' or 'look, there are some basic rules to storytelling that I think you should spend some time with, here maybe you could be mentored by this respected old dude.' And you realise that when they told you they wanted to support you to be radical, or political, or to challenge people, they actually didn't mean it. They might have even have thought they meant it, but they didn't. What they really meant was that they wanted you to be just enough of those things to be marketable and zeitgeisty, but no more. You know what I mean? To be the 'edginess' in their 'brand' but not to actually upset anyone, or take a risk. To be political enough to make people feel good about themselves for having 'engaged' but not to actually provoke anyone to do anything about anything. To actually just be comfortable and reassuring and safe. To stay safe. Because there's always a funding review around the corner and nobody can afford to fuck up.

Pause.

And so you stick at it, and tell yourself you've a lot to learn, and this is what you want so you better put the hours in. And you do alright. Enough to stay in work, just. And you move to London. Because that's what you do. And you notice that people are lovely there, but only when they think there is something they can get from you. And that's just how it works so you slowly, eventually fall into that just being how you relate to people. That's just what your relationships are.

Beat.

And the work is, fine.

Beat.

It's not gonna change anyone's life but it's fine. You reckon. Passable. You wind up on some training scheme seeking new talent to write by rote for a TV soap, telling yourself the rigour and the structure will be good for you or something. But you don't get the gig, because some part of you just cannot, *cannot* stick it. And you learn to hate that part. That part of you that wants something better than this. Than all of this. You viscerally hate it, and are disgusted by it, and are ashamed of it. Because that part is the part that's betraying you, that's making it impossible for you to keep going. But you know that you need to keep going if you're going to survive. Because there is a twenty year black hole in your CV that says all you know how to do, the only thing you know how to do, is make up fucking stories and hope that people like them. Only you're old now. And so nobody gives a fuck.

Beat.

And the world around you keeps getting worse. So much desperately terrifyingly worse. And you switch off from it, because you have to.

Beat.

Because it turns out that you need safety too, and reassurance. And so instead of trying to make things better or to do something real you just sit crying on the Tube and you don't know why. And eventually it dawns on you that this isn't what you ever thought this part of your life would look like or feel like. Sitting alone eating spaghetti hoops in the dark while your hair turns grey.

Beat.

Your agent stops getting in touch. Eventually you send him an email just to sort of wrap that thing up, make it official. And then you move back in with your mum. Who hates you, and will not speak to you. In a city where you've not lived for twenty-five years and where you're completely alone because you know no-one and no-one knows you. And after a while you notice that you've become one of those people who goes 'I'm a writer,' when actually, no honey – you're not. Not really. So you just stop saying it. And so you're not a writer. But you're not really anything else either.

Long pause.

Declan   Here, have you ever seen *Barton Fink*?

Libby   You've never heard of Pulp but you know about *Barton Fink*? What year were you born?

Declan   Two thousand and two.

Libby   Bloody hell.

Declan   What?

Libby   You're even younger than I thought.

Declan   What age are you like?

Libby   How'd you know about *Barton Fink*?

Declan   You're changing the subject.

Libby   No I'm not.

Declan   Netflix.

Libby   Of course.

Declan   And you?

Libby   I'm forty-six.

Declan   Fuck me.

Libby   What?

Declan   You're older than I thought.

Libby   Cheers. Well. Whatever you've seen in films, it's not all swanning around waiting for your muse to show up alright? It's work.

Declan   It's no actual work but is it.

Libby   It is. It might even make some people stinking rich. Mostly not though.

Declan   Why'd you even bother in the first place then?

Beat.

Libby   Would you believe me if I told you it was because I once thought that art and stories could change the world?

Declan   Ha. Nut.

Libby   Well, I did. I actually honestly did.

Declan   And. Why else?

Libby   Honest answer?

Declan *nods.*

Someone once told me I was good.

Beat.

Declan   You were actually gonnae jump eh?

Libby   I don't know.

Pause.

Declan   Right. The Modern Art hingmy. The one you said I'd like. Let's go tay that one.

Libby   Really?

Declan   Aye, fuck it eh, why no. It's no every day I get a pure tidy milf handing me her number eh, so –

Libby   That's really not –

Declan   I'm kidding you on!

Libby   Okay.

Beat.

Well. Two bacon rolls then?

Declan   Aye. Just brown sauce on mine though please.

Scene Seven

Projected text: Outside the Scottish National Gallery of Modern Art.

Libby   Well?

Declan *exhales long.*

Are you not going to say anything?

Declan   Unreal. Just absolutely unreal like.

Libby   Did you like it?

Declan   See they ones that were like these big weird bodies and these big mad shaped heids and that? Fucking hell. And the mouths. The big mad mental mouths.

Libby   Looks a bit like the stuff you draw right?

Declan   But up there. Like a proper art hing. I've never seen that, I've just never *seen that* before eh. What's his name again?

Libby   Francis Bacon.

Declan   Francis Bacon.

Beat.

Here, imagine your name was 'Bacon.' That's fucking mental. Big Frankie Bacon! Fucking Stevie Square Sausage. Billy Beans. What's next man?

Libby   Albert Avocado?

Declan   Ha! Big Albert Avocado, what a boy like. Here - can you really just come in here for free?

Libby   Yes of course.

Declan   That's fucking bonkers.

Libby   Well, it's yours. This place is yours. That's what I'm saying, it's for everyone.

Declan   Aye no really but. Did you no see that bouncer gadgie, pure looking at me, hinking I'm on the wind up –

Libby   He's not a bouncer Declan. He's an attendant. And they watch everyone like that.

Declan   Aye nae bother.

Libby   Hey, maybe your own work might be hung in a place like this one day –

Declan   I telt you. It's just daft pictures. Someone in the centre told me tae, said I should, said it'd help me. Thought fuck it, why no.

Libby   What's the centre?

Declan   Ach, they've closed it. Shut it doon noo.

Libby   That's why you draw up the Crags now then?

Declan   Went to the park at first. Polis noise you up for loitering but. So aye. Need it. Cos I get these like episodes eh – I'm no a fucking heidcase or that right? It's just fucking, like - I've Googled it. Said it's anxiety. Sure that's what it is, like stress. I'm meant tay avoid volatile situations, cos I get this like panic feeling eh, this – in my chest. Like a tightness. Like I'm drowning. And I fucking – tense up, and lash out, and, and, and the drawing just, like, helps me. Like, breathe. That's all it is. Dinnae show anycunt. No fucking chance. Gary's always making me out like I'm a total waster. Imagine he caught me daein this. Like a mentalist. Like some kinday fuckin fruit. Fuck that.

Libby   You've shown them to Siân though.

Declan   That's different. She's different. She gets it. And if Gary ever touches her I'll rip his fuckin tadger off eh.

Libby   Right.

Declan   Would like. Rip it off and chuck it in the sea man. Spit doon.

Libby   Okay.

Declan   Auld yin kens it. She gets it. She hates him an aw.

Libby   So why does she stay?

Declan   Nae choice. Cannae provide on her ain wi just shift work, so we've just got tae put up wi it and that's that. Ach, look, I'm no wanting to gie you some sob story or that –

Libby   I like stories.

Beat.

Libby   It all sounds – precarious. Like if one thing goes then –

Declan   I ken what precarious means, I'm no daft. I was at college.

Libby   What happened?

Declan   Booted off. Missing too many classes. Looking after the wee yin eh. My maw had shifts and Gary wouldnae dae it so that was that.

Libby   Right.

Declan   I dinnae hold it against her, eh. That's my job. I'm the big brother like, that's me. Teach her stuff, play games wi her and that. Show her karate. Just a loaday shite I've made up but she loves it man. Says I'll get her actual lessons one day. So that's the goal. Hard but.

Beat.

Libby   I see that.

Declan   Right.

Beat.

Listen I'm gonnae need to get back soon, eh –

Libby   No worries.

Declan   Thanks and that like. I mean –

Libby   No, no thank you.

Declan   Did you really – did you really think aboot they paintings an that when you looked at like – my drawings?

Libby   Absolutely. You liked them, right?

Declan   I did.

Beat.

Everything is going to be alright.

Libby   What?

Declan   Everything is going to be alright. Says it there, on the building. Big neon letters. Is that an art hing an aw, aye?

Libby   Yes. I suppose it is.

Declan   Fucking magic man.

Beat.

Here, sorry I dunno where all that stuff came fae, you cannae shut me up sometimes eh –

Libby   No. It's fine. I'm happy to hear it, I liked hearing it. I think you're – I think you're very brave.

Declan   Ha.

Beat.

I've got mair stories like that. If you want, like.

Scene Eight

Libby   At home I sit, looking up at Declan's picture. Plummy Radio Four voices bleed through the walls. Grey-haired public-school men, all measured tones, and reasonable empty words.

'Growth,' 'fairness,' 'economic uncertainty,' 'difficult decisions.' I look at Declan's picture. And I write. It just comes out. I write: *They've closed it. Shut it doon noo.*

Libby *writes. Projected text reads*: They've closed it. Shut it doon noo.

Declan *reaches for his box of pencils. He draws.*

Projected text, the following phrases, as **Libby** *writes:*

I dinnae hold it against her eh. She's different. She gets it.

In my chest. Like a tightness. Like I'm drowning.

I ken what precarious means, I'm no daft.

Scene Nine

Projected text: A battered graffiti-marked bus stop. Dusk.

Declan   Am I gonna have to act? Cos I cannae act –

Libby   Just be yourself. I shouldn't have switched this on really, it's just for notes. Just ignore it – just be you.

Declan   Is this is like an interview then?

Libby   Just think of it like a conversation.

Declan   Right.

Beat.

And it's gonnae be a play aboot me?

Libby   Not necessarily. Inspired by. Maybe. It's really not anything yet, just – thoughts and ideas.

Pause.

Do you remember, Declan, when you were asking what a play was and I –

Declan   Aye, well I knew what it *was* like, I was just –

Libby   For sure. Sure. But you wanted to know what the point was?

Declan   Aye.

Libby   Well I've been asking that myself – because you asked me – what's the point? Because there is one. In spite of all the shite. And it's hard to describe but I think it's this: watching a theatre performance, an audience's heart beat synchronises.

Beat.

Declan   Is that it?

Libby   Yeah.

Declan   Right –

Libby   See, normally – in our normal, daily lives – our heart beats are totally isolated from each other. But in the theatre, our individual pulses will speed up and slow down at the same time, as we feel something – as we laugh, or cry, or even just something smaller than that, on the inside. And sometimes – because we're here, we're here together in the same room – the rhythm of our heart beats will actually fall in synch.

Declan   That's pretty mental.

Libby   That's science. See when it works, it is like this huge empathy machine. And if I – if we – can take a story, a voice like yours and put it into that machine. And for people to listen. To listen to you. Your story. I think – well. I think that could be really something. I think that could be the point.

Beat.

Great. So just ignore this. And we'll just go for a walk. Round here. And have a chat.

Declan   Right.

Beat.

Let me dae all the talking if we bump intay anyone right, it's very, very dangerous.

Libby   Okay. Okay, thank you.

Declan   Ha ha! Fucking hell I'm yanking yer chain, fucksake!

Scene Ten

Libby, *listening to recordings. She begins to type. Projected text*:
awright wee yin?

Declan   Awright wee yin? Want tay play at karate? She doesnae
want tay play at karate. She's just curled up in the corner, silent,
listening to the fucking racket through the walls. Gary screaming
about how I'm a drain on this house how I'm a disgrace, a selfish
disgrace, he'll no put up wi having me around much longer. Auld
yin's saying sorry, sorry, sorry. I'm sorry. Actually fucking
apologising tae the cunt for the state ay me like.

Touch my lip, and it's red on my hands. The wee yin sees it.
What's that Declan, she says. That blood? I goes, aye. Fake blood
darlin. Fae the ghost shop. Practicing. For Halloween ken? Want
tay play at drawing pictures? Let's play at drawing pictures. Fuck
they two through there eh, fuck em. So I gets oot Libby's posh
pencils and the wee yin's drawing and making up stories. I asks
her, what's that one? She says it's a dragon. And then she's like
that, and this one here is a man made oot ay cheese. That one's for
you. Fucking magic man. And she goes, what's yours like? Well
what do you hink it is wee yin? She goes it's a man on a big stage.
That's right I says – I'd drawn a big theatre wi curtains and
everything. What's he daein, she says. He's tellin everyone his
story darling. I think he's happy. Is that right? Why's that? She
says cause look, aw these people are listening tay him and clapping
and telling him he's good. Well, maybe he is happy I says. Maybe
he is. She says your fake blood looks real Declan. I goes aye. It's
good stuff. You can get fake stuff that looks just like the real stuff.
Now get intae yer jammies it's past your bedtime. Cuddle her
doon. Try and get her tay sleep.

Got working on this big massive yin, right. Fucking class man.
Been working on it for days and days. The boy on the stage like I

drew for the wee yin but I've added like this big ginormous mental mouth. Opening right up and there's all madness spilling oot. Pictures ay the scheme, the flats, people and that like gushing oot. And mixed in wi all the chaos and madness and violence, if you look for it, coming out ay the same mouth you can see the words: everything is going to be alright. Libby's pure intae it, she's like:

Libby   I really liked that one you did, the mouth piece.

Declan   So that's what I've called it. *Mouthpiece*. Giein it a name like it's an actual hing. Signed it an everything. Even stuck it on the fucking wall man. Actual. Gary sees it eh. Tears it doon, obviously. Kent he would. He's like fucks this? I pick it up. Dinnae say anyhin. Just stick it back tae the wall eh. Cunt didnae like that, not one bit. Squares up, pushes me like that, the fuck is this. I gies him a dunt back. Just a wee fucking dunt, like that. Aye that's surprised him. Never saw that coming did he the old prick. I point to the picture and I says, the fuck is what, Gary? The fuck is this? This, I says. Look him square in the eye. This here is an artwork called *Mouthpiece*. By me: Declan fucking Swan.

Scene Eleven

Projected text: Salisbury Crags. Night time. Declan and Libby sit. Declan rolls a spliff with cheap hash resin.

Declan *and* **Libby** *sit, talking and laughing together*.

Libby   Oh, it's hard to explain. Like sometimes it's just easier if you like channel someone else. When you're stuck. Hey – you know Courtney Love?

Declan   Nut.

Libby   Oh come on! Kurt Cobain? Nirvana?

Declan   Aye, cunt wi the shades. Black and white. On they goth t-shirts.

Libby   Right. So she was his – they were like together –

Declan   Did she no shoot him in the face?

Libby   No.

Declan   Pretty sure I heard she shot him in the face like.

Libby   No, that's not what – what about Michael Stipe? R.E.M.?

Declan   Nope.

Libby   Ooft. Mental.

Declan   Well, mibbe, aye. Though failure to identify nineties pop stars probably wouldnae be part ay any official diagnosis or that.

Libby   Here, if we're being literal about it then I'm the one on fucking meds –

Declan   That doesnay mean anything. It's 2019 pal everycunt is on anti-depressants.

Libby   Fair.

Declan   I'm only fucking you about.

Libby   Yeah, you're good at that.

Declan   Ken.

Libby   Tease.

Declan *lights the spliff. He offers it to* **Libby**. **Libby** *shakes her head.* **Declan** *smokes.*

Libby   Some view, eh?

Declan   Uh huh.

Beat.

Libby   Changed my mind. Here.

Libby *takes the spliff, inhales and coughs.*

Declan   Gies that then.

Declan *takes* **Libby**'s *flask and drinks from it. He sprays it out.*

Fuck even *is* that?

Libby   Gin. It's my mum's. She's an alcoholic.

Declan   Eh, naw she's no. Folk like you urnae alcoholics. My da, he was an alcoholic.

Libby   I've never heard you mention him before.

Declan   My da topped himsel when I was seven.

Libby   Oh. I'm sorry.

Declan   It's cool. I'm no. It's cool.

Declan *drinks.*

Gary always says I'm gonnae end up just like him. Everycunt says it. Like it's written oot for me. How I ruin everything and I'm only gonnae cause cunts pain. Just like my da. But I'm no. Put that doon. Where's that recorder hingmy?

Libby   It's not on.

Declan   You no recording nut?

Libby   No.

Declan   Right.

Pause.

So what about this Courtney wifey?

Libby   Oh, I dunno. I cannae mind.

Declan   'Cannae mind.' Ha ha, class.

Libby   What? I'm from Edinburgh too you know.

Declan   Aye, you're speaking like that cos you're talking tae me but eh? Bet you're one ay they cunts who talks different to taxi drivers an that eh. Ha ha. Boy comes roond tae fix your boiler you're like that, dropping the t's calling him 'mate' an 'pal' an that.

Libby   I totally do do that.

Declan *laughs.*

Fuck off. It's a totally normal thing. It's just – human. I bet you don't talk to me the way you talk to Gary do you –

Declan   Right right, right finish your story then!

Libby   No. I'm not telling you now.

Declan   Oh come on! I want tae ken.

Libby   I can't remember.

Declan   Come on. Courtney –

Declan *gets his pencils and paper out. He draws as* **Libby** *talks.*

Libby   Courtney Love. She said this thing in an interview. That sometimes when she's onstage dancing or whatever she gets a bit . . . stuck. Rock block, I suppose. She's there in front of thousands of people all singing along and she just – freezes. And she says in those moments, what she does is she channels Michael Stipe. She goes, how would Michael dance to this – and then does that. And that gets her through, and she's back in it, doing her thing. Like he helps her find herself.

Declan   Right.

Libby   I love that. That we draw on each other, for help. When we're lost. We can reach out, borrow from each other's – I dunno – essence to help us find our own. We're not separate. We're all pissing in and drinking from the same trough.

Declan   That is pure clingin.

Beat.

Nice to be writing again then, aye?

Libby   Uh huh. Maybe even get someone to read it, what do you think?

Declan   And I take it you must be the Courtney lassie in that story aye?

Libby   What?

Declan   And the dancing boy. Michael gadgie. That's me is it?

Libby   Mibbe.

Declan   Ha. Tidy! Never been compared tae a rock star before eh. 'Rawk stah!' Yas.

Libby *laughs.* **Declan** *draws.*

Libby   Show me?

Declan   Nut. It's no finished.

Libby   You'll need new pencils at this rate. And I'll make you a playlist. Pulp. R.E.M. Nirvana. And Hole.

Declan   'Hole?'

Libby   Yes.

Declan   Heh heh.

Libby   Fucksake.

Declan   Sorry. Gies that.

Declan *takes the spliff and smokes.*

Do you think maybe, next time, instead ay like a gallery we could go and see what you do? Like a play?

Libby   Are you asking me to take you to the theatre?

Declan   Mibbe.

Libby   Well get you.

Beat.

You do know I've not actually been to the theatre in a very long time don't you?

Declan   So?

Beat.

Libby   Alright. Fucking brilliant. Yes. Yes let's do this. Definitely.

Declan   Cool.

Beat.

Libby   Declan?

Declan   What?

Libby *plays music from here phone.*

Fuck's that?

Libby   Hole.

Declan   Shite.

Declan *keeps drawing,* **Libby** *bops her head to the music, singing along. She starts dancing.* **Declan** *laughs.*

Fuck you playing at ya mentalist!

Libby   Dance with me.

Declan   Fuck off!

Libby   Come on.

She pulls **Declan** *up on to his feet. They laugh. She dances.*

Come on!

Declan *joins in, bopping about like a joker.*

Projected text: Declan dances. Libby dances. They dance and laugh together as the city lights up below them.

Scene Twelve

Libby *steps out of the scene. She watches* **Declan**.

Libby   The midpoint. The clue is in the title really; this bit is about halfway through. Depending on the story you're telling, everything at this point should be either brilliant, or terrible. If it's brilliant it's because your main relationship is contented and your characters appear to have everything they want and need from each other. If it's terrible, then it's because they don't. The image at the midpoint should be a reversal of how the story will end, if you're really playing it to the letter of the law. So if at this point things are really shit, don't worry because it probably means that – you know – they'll pick up. And if things are really good at this bit then, maybe – well maybe they're not going to stay that way forever.

Libby *steps back into the scene. She and* **Declan** *dance with wild abandon. The music cuts out.*

Scene Thirteen

Projected text: I'm still a bit baked tae be honest.

Declan   I'm still a bit baked tae be honest, still a bit spaced oot when I get back hame. Expect tae find Gary and my maw there. But in the kitchen it's no Gary and my maw. It's just my maw. Sat there on her todd.

Where's Gary? She doesnae look up.

Where's Gary? So she looks up this time. She's been crying. Mascara aw doon her face, she says it's your fault Declan.

Fuck you on aboot, what is?

It's your fault. You ken he was already at the end ay his tether wi you. No paying your way. But you had tae make it worse didn't you. Acting all uppitty. Sneaking out tae see whoever it is you're sneaking off tae see, undermining him. You Declan. Embarrassing him. Sticking up your stupid fucking pictures tae humilitae him, making a big fucking stink around the place, well well fucking done she says. Cos noo he's gone. He's gone and he's no coming back.

Is he deid like?

Naw he's no fucking deid dipstick! He left! He wasnae fucking joking. He's done it. That's it. He's gone.

Mum, I says. Mum this is, this is, he's a bad fucking cunt eh – dae you know think a ken what he does tae you? This is good –

Don't you fucking dare tell me what is good. For us, when I'm the one who has to figure out how we fucking *survive*, don't you dare!

Projected text: Where's Siân? Where's Siân?

But Mum's turned away. She's no even blinking. Like she's done wi me. So I dive intae the room. Tae find the wee yin.

Siân? Siân? She's lying in bed in the dark, totally still. But I can tell that she's awake.

Have you been greeting? What have they said tae you? What has she been saying tae you? But she's no talking, she just stares at me. For ages. And then she goes:

Projected text: Declan. Aye?

Projected text: I don't love them.

Dinnae say that wee yin, course you do.

Projected text: I love you but.

Beat.

Projected text: You'll not leave me alone with them, will you?

Listen. Listen, Siân. Look at me wee yin, look at me. Everything is going to be alright. Hear that? Everything is going to be alright. Say it.

Everything is going to be alright.

Projected text: Everything is going to be alright.

Scene Fourteen

Libby   I hadn't expected to feel so fucking terrified. Like I'm suddenly worried about being seen here or something. It's completely stupid, it's just some daft touring comedy thing at the King's Theatre. But still. It's the feeling. So I sit in the bar and order myself a drink.

I try calling him, but nothing. The bell goes and the bar starts to empty. An usher sees the tickets on my table and says all friendly that I'd better be heading over, but I suddenly realise that I don't want to be doing this on my own at all – and I don't know how to say that to this nice woman so I just look at her and say nothing and smile weirdly at her and then stand up leaving the tickets on the table and walk out of the building. Bloody hell. It's raining and I don't know what I'm doing anymore so I head into Bennett's Bar and have another drink.

A couple of hours later Declan texts me. It just says:

Projected text: Sorry. Then another, it says:

Projected text: You could come here? For fucksake Declan.

Projected text: Please.

Scene Fifteen

Projected text: Declan's bedroom. Night.

Declan *hands her a can.*

Declan   Sorry it's Tennent's.

Libby   I like Tennent's.

Pause.

Is there somewhere I can put my coat?

Declan   Oh – aye course. Sorry. Just. Put it anywhere like.

Libby *looks around. She chucks the coat on the bed. She sits.*

Libby   This is – her bed? Siân?

Declan   Aye. I'm on the roll matt. Till I get my ain place like.

Declan *drinks.*

Libby   And they're – where are they?

Declan   Fuck knows. Maw's pal's hoose, probably. She doesnae tell me fuck aw anymair. Writes wee messages sometimes. 'Buy milk.' 'Buy fags.' 'Get a job.' That's it but.

Libby   Right.

Long pause.

And Gary. Do you know where he went to?

Declan   Naw.

Libby   Right.

Pause.

Well. Maybe it's a good thing. It's probably a good thing, right?

Declan *drinks. Pause.*

Libby   It's not your fault, Declan.

Declan *sobs.*

It's not.

Declan   He's right. He's fucking right. Aboot me.

Libby   He's not, Declan. He's not. None of this is your fault, you have done nothing wrong.

Declan   Fucking useless, fucking hopeless fucking stupid cunt.

Libby   Declan.

Declan *sobs.* **Libby** *sits closer to him.*

I'm here. It's okay.

Declan *leans closer in to* **Libby***, sobbing.*

I'm here. Take a deep breath.

Declan   I'm just a fucking waste.

Libby   No –

Declan   I am but –

Libby   Declan, no. You are not. You are not.

Declan *sobs.*

Declan, when I got home the night we met do you know what I did?

Declan *shakes his head.*

Libby   I leaned over the bathroom sink and I drank bucket- loads of tap water, and I let it run down my chin and my clothes and it tasted amazing. Then I jumped in the shower and scrubbed and scrubbed until my skin was pink and tingly and hot and sore. Know why?

Beat.

Because I might not have seen the next day. And if I was going to then I wanted to step into it new. In new skin. I didn't want to play games anymore. No more shite. If I was going to continue then I was going to do something that mattered. I was going to do something that *mattered* and that is why I came to speak to *you* –

Declan *kisses* **Libby** *on the mouth.* **Libby** *sits back, alarmed. They look at each other. She kisses him back.*

Declan   Is this – is this, I dunno, is this – is this okay, that we're doing this? Is –

Libby   Yes. Yes. Yes it is.

Beat.

It really is.

Declan *kisses* **Libby**. *More confidently. Their making-out becomes more urgent, more frantic, more desperate.* **Libby** *hurriedly unfastens her belt, her jeans. It is passionate and determined.* **Libby** *puts her hand into* **Declan***'s tracky bottoms, she thrusts her hand.*

I can go slower if you want –

Libby *looks at* **Declan**. *She thrusts her hand some more.* **Declan** *lies still.*

Declan   It's cool, it's cool just gie it – I'll get there like –

Libby *thrusts.*

Libby   Is it?

Declan   Aye.

Libby *thrusts. Then stops. They look at each other. She removes her hand from his tracky bottoms.*

Declan   I'm just – I'm just a wee bit nervous eh.

Beat.

Libby   You've never done this before have you?

Beat.

Declan   Sorry.

Libby   Right. Okay. This was – this was weird. And daft. Um. Right –

Declan   I want tae eh! I just –

Libby   Right. No. I think we – I think we shouldn't, actually. Probably.

Libby *fastens her belt up. Silence.*

This is isn't your fault Declan.

Declan *says nothing. He puts his head in his hands, avoiding eye contact.*

Please don't be embarrassed. You really shouldn't be embarrassed, you've done nothing to be embarrassed about. Really I'm the one who should be embarrassed. Not that I'm embarrassed, I mean. I didn't mean that I'm embarrassed to – that's not what – oh fucking hell.

Pause.

Right. Right right right. Okay. I – I should probably. Be going. I think. Don't you?

Beat.

It's not your fault.

Beat.

Sorry. I'm sorry, Declan.

Libby *leaves.*

Declan   Fuck!

Declan *kicks the wall. He punches himself in the head, hard.*

Fuck!

Declan *hits himself again, repeatedly. Harder, and harder, and harder.*

Fuck! Fuck! Fuck! Fuck!

Scene Sixteen

Libby *is at her laptop, unable to write.* **Declan** *is on the phone.*

Libby   Some things are just rules. And they're worth paying attention to, if you're stuck.

Declan   Libby. It's me. Gonnae just pick up?

Declan *hangs up. He calls again.*

Libby   Your protagonist should meet some kind of reversal or obstacle around two thirds to three quarters of the way through. Something which fundamentally raises the stakes of the relationship.

Declan   Libby. For fucksake. Can you just call me back? Please.

He hangs up.

Libby   So, you know. Do that.

Libby *stares at her screen. She slams the laptop shut.*

Scene Seventeen

Projected text: A café. Edinburgh New Town. Weeks later.

Libby   Declan. I owe you an apology. I should never have let this happen. I should have been more – professional. From the start. It was my responsibility to look after – look I'm a fucking idiot. Okay?

Declan   I missed you.

Libby   I know. I've missed you too.

Declan   See last time, I'm sorry it just took me by surprise it's no that –

Libby   It's okay. We're not going to talk about that. I did try to be very clear on the phone about that.

Declan   Sure. Cool. Take it slow. It was all a bit ay rush I thought so –

Libby   That's not – we're not taking anything slow. Okay? I like you Declan, I think you're a special, person but – there isn't a future like that. For us. Okay? I'd love if we could just – go back to how it was. Except this time, maybe for everyone's sake, we need to lay some ground rules. Something we really should have done – *I* should have done – at the start. Okay? I know it might feel weird but – it'll be better. It really will be better. I promise.

Right. First. We really need to start making a distinction between time as friends, and time that's work. And right now, we're meeting to talk about the play. Alright? Second. You can always stop talking when you want to. I don't want to force you to do anything or say anything. Third. We don't talk about what happened last time. Not again. Not when I'm recording, and certainly not to anyone else. Have you told anyone else?

Declan   Christ. It's no like it makes you a paedo or that, fucking hell man.

Libby   Declan.

Declan   I'm just saying. Can women even be paedos? Doubt it.

Libby   Declan, please. This is serious. What happened last time was a mistake and you have to forget it. Can I be any clearer? Whatever permission, whatever invitation you think – get rid of it. Declan? My consent. I withdraw my consent. Do you get what that means?

Declan *nods.*

Okay. Now, if you want me to leave that's okay, I'll respect that. Do you want me to go?

Declan *shakes his head.*

Right then.

Pause.

Are you okay, Declan? Are you coping okay?

Declan   I suppose you want to hear some good stories aboot poverty an that now aye?

Beat.

Libby   I really did want to know that you're okay.

Declan   I'm fine.

Pause.

Libby   So, about the play. I've got some thoughts. And I'd like to share them with you. It's just an idea. For the end. And I wanted to talk to you about it to see if you thought it felt – I don't know – truthful, I suppose.

Libby *takes out a manuscript.*

Declan   'Mouthpiece: a play by Libby Quinn.' Dae I no get a mention, naw?

Libby   Of course, I'm writing an author's note. It'll be pretty extensive –

Declan   That named after my drawing aye?

Libby   Yes, well, it's a phrase that shows up at various points in the script. You can read it. I'd be very, very happy for you to read it. It's just a draft, we can add things. But the ending, I know it might be a bit sensitive, so –

Declan   I top masel don't I?

Libby   Not you. The character. The character in the play does, yes.

Declan   You're joking?

Libby   No.

Declan *laughs.*

What's so funny?

Declan   So what, take a cunt like me right, make him top himsel cause ay the bad poverty. Tragedy. Poor cunt like me. An aw the cunts like *you* sit there and go 'very sad, aye, very bad, tut tut, oh dear.'

Libby   That's not what I'm doing. You know that's not – we've spoken about this. Everyone who has read it thinks the ending is actually successful, so –

Declan   Who the fuck else has read it like?

Libby   A theatre. Just some people at a theatre –

Declan *laughs.*

I thought you'd be pleased.

Declan   'Oh look at these disturbing drawings, boy must be a right heidcase, eh? Aye. Right good for a drama but! Look this one's called *Mouthpiece* let's name it that, the mad mental bastard!'

Libby   The title has multiple meanings.

Declan   Does it aye?

Libby   And the ending is –

Declan   I understand, dinnae worry. A necessary sacrifice. And we aw learn a big important lesson. And we're aw very pleased for ourselves.

Libby   This happens, this is a real thing that really happens, and it's happening more and more –

Declan   You ken it disnae work like that but eh? Cunts dinnae just top themsels in big dramatic moments. At the end ay something. It happens at some random point in a long slow process ay shite. It happens quietly. And naebody fucking cares. But I suppose you wouldnae ken aboot that, would you? You just *slipped*.

Libby   Whoa. Okay. Look, if I can just explain. Please. I tell stories. Alright? That's all I can do. I want this story, your story to be heard, Declan. To be noticed. That's what matters. There are certain rules to storytelling okay? And what we're talking about is the final image. And a good final image needs to resolve the themes, and –

Declan   Fuck dae I care?

Libby   Declan. I'm trying to do the right thing by you here. I really – I think this is good. People need this if they're going to listen. I need to tell a dramatic story. It needs a resolution. And what we've got here is too important, this message –

Declan   Message? The fucking message? Telling me what I can and cannae talk aboot, handing oot your fucking rules. Saying you want tae listen tae me, get ma voice heard but look: you've already written my end. Just like every. Other. Cunt. Well fuck you.

Libby   I think you're being a little bit unreasonable.

Declan   Unreasonable? This is unreasonable? Ken whit, you can fuck off then and say ta-ta to your skanky 'project' cos I'm fucked if I'm letting you use my story.

Libby   Well. You can't just simply do that all of a sudden, that's not –

Declan   Fucking watch me. Here: I withdraw my consent. You like that?

Libby   Come on that's different. That is different.

Declan   How?

Beat.

Libby   Because. This is my story now.

Declan   But you needed me.

Libby *goes to leave.*

Ach, fuck ye then!

Libby   I'm sorry Declan, I really am.

Declan   Well away tae fuck then ya dirty old cow! Hope you die in a bin fire ya fucking slag man! Hear that? I'll dae it masel, swear doon! Cut you up ya slut! Here that's a joke by the way! No for real! Or is it? Eh? Ha ha fucking write that intay yer play ya cunt!

Scene Eighteen

Libby   Declan keeps calling. But I don't pick up.

When I stopped replying by text, he tried the landline. Endlessly. I had to unplug it. Told my mum it was because we were getting too many PPI calls. But she knew. And one day, at the kitchen table, she just reached out and held my arm. And kept her hand there for a bit. Then walked off.

Of course, then she said her fucking stupid condescending thing, she said 'you're not a social worker love.' But to be honest – she's right.

Start to see a therapist. And it's good. Tell her about Declan. How I miss him. She understands, but when I show her his pictures and his messages she's very clear that it's not healthy for him to be part of my life just now. And, I must say, I'm inclined to agree with her that navigating weird feelings about the teenager I tried to give a handjob to in his five-year-old sister's bed is not a fantastic look for a person trying to find her way out of a mid-life crisis.

Met a few guys on Tinder. Wankers mostly. But one's okay. He's called Brian. He works in HR for Scottish Widows. He's nice. He's really into comics, which is fine I suppose. And his profile isn't full of spelling and grammar mistakes or stupid statements like he 'enjoys fun.' I've not let him see anything I'm writing yet and he's not pushy, which I like.

The last text I get from Declan is just two words. But I understand it completely. It just says:

Projected text: they've gone.

Libby   I want to tell him that he's not alone. I want to help. But sometimes the right thing is the hardest thing. And I need to start doing this right. I owe it to him. To be clear. And professional. So I reply:

Projected text: Declan I am truly sorry. Please seek support from someone who can help you. A professional perhaps. One of those numbers I sent you. I cannot be that person.

Libby   Change my number. And that's that. He's gone.

I look back over all the transcripts, the recordings, listen to the voicemails, read the draft material about Siân. The wee yin. To try to put into words. His words. What it means – right now – to lose her. But I can't of course I can't. Instead, I write: *Declan sits in his bedroom, head in his hands.*

Projected text: Declan sits in his bedroom, head in his hands.

Declan *sits in his bedroom, head in his hands.*

Libby   I write: *Slowly, silently his body begins to shake.*

Projected text: Slowly, silently his body begins to shake.

Slowly, silently his body begins to shake.

Libby   I write: *He punches his bed. He punches himself in the head.*

Projected text: He punches his bed. He punches himself in the head.

He punches his bed. He punches himself in the head.

Libby   I write: *He tears down his picture; the man telling his story. He rips it into tiny pieces.*

Projected text: He tears down his picture; the man telling his story. He rips it into tiny pieces.

He tears down his picture; the man telling his story. He rips it into tiny pieces.

Libby   I write: *He takes out a small pocket knife and stabs the pillow.*

Projected text: He takes out a small pocket knife and stabs the pillow.

He takes out a small pocket knife and stabs the pillow.

Libby   I write: He screams.

Projected text: He screams.

He screams.

Libby   I write: *Slumped on the floor, Declan sobs, alone.*

Projected text: Slumped on the floor, Declan sobs, alone.

Slumped on the floor, **Declan** *sobs, alone.*

Scene Nineteen

Declan   Ken that feeling like you're hurtling tae the bottom and you just cannae stop?

My maw's note said sorry. Said she understands Gary's no perfect but he offered some security. Said she wouldnae leave an address but she'd try tae phone sometimes.

Getting moved on by the housing, obviously. Good. Pure creepy being here when it's empty. Mingin. The smell an that. The silence. I sleep on the mat still eh cause it's easier sometimes just tae pretend, ken?

Hudnae drawn for months. Just sitting here, staring oot. I wisnae gonnae just fucking greet aboot it. Right? I needed tae dae something eh. Take matters intae my ain hands.

Picked up a newspaper on a bus seat right. And fucking guess whO's in it. Libby. Talking aboot her play. *Mouthpiece.* It's coming up, at the Traverse Theatre in toon. The newspaper piece is all aboot how since moving back she's rediscovered her voice. It says it's an urgent portrait of another side to Edinburgh, from the front

line of Britain's poverty crisis. Says she's 'a mouthpiece for
generation austerity, a voice for the lost and the voiceless, a truly
authentic voice.' So there you go eh. Good for her.

Got a missed call fae a withheld number. Voicemail. The wee yin.
Saying she wants to learn more karate moves and would I like to
come to her sixth birthday party. I hear Gary in the background.
The wee yin tells me to come and see her soon. And then hangs up.
She never left a number. Fuck man!

She'd ring back like eh? Next time I'd answer. Next time, when she
called, I'd pick up and I'd tell her that things wirnae gonnae stay
this way. That everything was going to be alright. That I had a plan.

Security. That's what the auld yin said.

I'd seen in that paper there was a thing where the play had a
question and answer hingmy. Where you could go. Tae ask the
writer your questions. I needed tae take action. I kent who I needed
tae speak tae. I kent where I was gonnae go tae get this fixed.

I was goin tae the fuckin theatre.

Scene Twenty

Projected text: Traverse Theatre, Edinburgh. Night.

Libby   Opening night. Brian comes. And so does Mum. She
doesn't try to mix with me, and I'm glad she doesn't. But I'm glad
she's here.

The theatre's arranged invites, industry folk. I've seen the list. All
these names, organisations, even folk who'd have been more likely
to look at me if I was shit on their shoe – they're here. And they
know my name, and act like we've all been pals for ages. And
they're speaking to me in the bar. Asking what I'm going to do
next. And I smile, and shake their hands. And it feels nauseating
but suddenly there's this faint whiff of a possibility that things
won't ever have to go back to the way they were. And I'm not
going to let myself fuck that up.

Declan   Standing outside. So many fucking people cutting aboot the place. I walk towards the big shiny sign: *Traverse Theatre*. Doors open. I step in. The walk up to the desk is long like, and the floor makes a noise like walking up the corridor to a head teacher's office. These three people at the end. Students or that, no much older than me like. They all look up. I dinnae ken which one I'm meant tae speak tae so I just stand there eh like a fuckin prize dick. One ay the lassies looks at me aw smiley so I goes an explains tay her, I says, sorry – I'm here for the eh – the theatre. She goes, which show?

There's a poster behind her. Boy in a hoody, wi his fucking mouth scratched out. Fucksake. And these drawings around him, all bits ay Edinburgh, like what I draw. Like my drawings. Stuck up on a wall in a place like this. I point tae it and says that one. She says *Mouthpiece*? I says aye. That's the one.

She asks if I'm paying by cash or card. I says I thought it was free. She just stares at me eh. Shakes her heid. I says I thought – I'm sorry, it's just someone telt me these places like this were free, cos, cos they're for everyone. She looks at me like I'm mental eh. She says I'm sorry I don't know why anyone told you that, that's not true. I ask her how much it is and she says it's fifteen pounds. Fifteen fucking pound! I start counting out ma coins. Sorry, I says. Sorry, I've never come here before eh. She adds it up and it's seven pound twenty. I tell her that's it. That's aw I've got.

She says are you a concession, I says I dunno. She says well are you unemployed, I says aye. Have you got proof? I says, naw. I dinnae. Then she smiles, prints off a ticket and says, don't worry. On you go.

Thank you, I say. Thank you, thank you, thank you.

Libby   I sit. Watching the audience, the press, all file in. Oh Christ. Oh fuck.

Declan   We aw file intay the room. I keep the hood up, heid doon. Pluck for somewhere near the back, try tae just keep it on the down low like. Just keep my heid the gether. Keep my eye on the prize.

Libby   It's your flesh and your blood up there. Whatever anyone says. Not just your voice, it's your heart. And your soul. Under the scrutiny and judgement of hundreds of eyes.

Declan   And I'm sitting here eh, surrounded by aw yous cunts. And then the lights go dark. And everyone shuts up. And listens.

Libby   Like sitting in the public stalls of your own trial and execution.

And it's over.

Declan   It's aw there eh. Siân. Gary. Me. Except no me. They even got a wee fucking ginger cunt tae play me, I'm no fucking ginger man, fucksake!

Libby   And they clap.

Declan   Every cunt just starts clapping.

Libby   I take a big drink. Steady the ship.

Declan   Keep it the gether. Stick tae the fucking game plan Declan.

Libby   Check my notes. Check for shaky hands. Get the game face on. Breathe. Smile.

Declan   A lassie in a black t-shirt walks on tae the stage. Tells us there's gonnae be a talk-back with the writer in aboot fifteen minutes so you've time tae get to the bar. I'm no going fucking anywhere. This next bit was what I came for. The talk-back. Tae talk back.

Libby   I take my seat, on the stage. And you're all looking at me. And the lights are hot and it's hard to see you.

Declan   And there she is. Right there. No seen her in ages. She looks like – happy. And safe. And calm.

Libby   And you all clap. And I don't know what to do so I just – try to smile back.

Declan   She's there. She's right there.

Libby   I say I wanted to tell a story that would make people take notice. How I wanted to respond to the way the world really is. How close to my heart the story is.

Declan   Libby.

Libby   The director says, it's a love story really though, isn't it? And I say, yes. Yes I suppose that's right.

Declan   Then they're talking aboot the ending. How 'tragic' it was. The wee arsehole who plays me pipes up – honestly he's been speaking like me for the last hour and a half, pipes up noo in this wee chirpy cunty voice and says it's very 'meta.'

Libby   They talk about the blood. How real it looked. How it really did look like the real thing.

Declan   Fuck this man – naw! I stick up my hand.

Libby   We'll take questions at the end.

Declan   I stand up.

Libby   Oh fuck.

Declan   I speak.

Libby   Oh fuck.

Declan   Hiya Libby.

Libby   Declan.

Declan   You remember me aye?

Libby   Declan, I – it's. It's great that you're here. I – thank you. Thank you. For coming.

Declan   Congratulations, eh. It was – good.

Libby   Oh. Good.

Declan   I – I've missed you like.

Libby   I've missed you too.

Beat.

I'm sorry – everyone I should explain, this is Declan and –

Declan   Hiya ladies and gentlemen. Enjoying your drinks aye? Um. Hing is right. My name is Declan Swan and this play stole my life –

Libby   Oh shit.

Declan   Someone laughs. Like this was a joke.

Libby   Okay. Okay, Declan, it's good you're here. It is. Everyone, this – This is a wonderful honour. For us all. You see Declan is – there's no other way of putting it –

Declan   She says how I'm the real life cunt fae the play, how I'm her inspiration. How she couldnae have done it without me. And suddenly, everyone's fucking pleased tae see me. The host wifey asks me is that true? And I just nod. Cause it is! It fucking is! And yous are clapping. Clapping for – me.

Libby   Game face. Keep smiling. Breathe.

Declan   Everycunt's buzzin eh. The actor laddie steps up and shakes ma hand. I shake it and grip it just a wee bit too tight, ginger cunt. He says make sure we live tweet this, the real star's arrived. And I mind the drawing I did for the wee yin. The boy in the theatre, and how he' happy – Naw! Here it wisnae aw like that by the way! What it is right – I dae drawings, right, and Libby liked them so – look it's no like I'm some radge cunt!

Libby   Declan.

Declan   I needed tae see you Libby. I didnae have anyone else tae –

Libby   We can talk about all this later, okay?

Declan   Okay. Aye. Cause it's all fucking very well wanting to be a voice for the voiceless eh. Until you find oot the voiceless have a fucking voice and mibbe they might want tay use it.

Beat.

Aye, that's fucking shut yous up.

Libby   Later Declan. Please.

Declan   No. Now.

Libby   I'm sorry if I hurt you. I hope you can understand, that now is not –

Declan   You've all seen the play right? You've aw seen how I – how my gadgie in the play – how I need. Security. Security, right? For the wee yin. Tae get her back.

Libby   Declan.

Declan   I needed to see you.

Libby   What is it you want?

Beat.

Declan   Money.

Libby   What?

Beat.

Declan   Nine grand.

Libby   Declan for fucksake you can't be serious.

Declan   Deadly mate. Nine grand, that's what you get for writing a play, that's what you said. My story. My words. You just said. So I'd like some money please.

Libby   Declan. Listen to me.

Declan   Sounds precarious. Aye. Well it is. Security, that's the hing. That's aw they left for. So get the money, get the security, get the wee yin back. Pay for her karate, get her a birthday present and then – me and you can work together Libby, we can –

Libby   Declan –

Declan   Or else there's nothing. For me. Actually *nothing*. Do you understand?

Libby   Declan –

Declan   I saw this was on and I thought, she'll be there. And I thought well, I have tae be there too.

Libby   Declan, look at me. We're finishing this now okay –

Declan   Naw, I'm no finished! I'm no finished with the talk-back!

Libby   That's all the time we have. It's over. Let's go somewhere and talk this out. Okay?

Declan   We can talk here. In the theatre. That's what we've been daein. A big fucking empathy machine eh, am I right? Am I fucking right? I said I'm still talking.

Libby   Declan, no.

Declan *punches himself in the head.*

Declan, stop it!

Declan *punches himself in the head.*

Declan!

Declan *punches himself in the head.*

Stop it now!

Declan   I said! I'm still! Talking! And you're going tae fucking listen! Tae me!

Declan *pulls out a pocket knife.*

Declan   I've got mair stories. Libby. I've got them. Loads. Fucking loads. We could, we could dae like – we could dae a TV series or that. One lump sum now, I'll gie you – everything. My life from now on – it's yours. Look. Look here, look – it's fuckin good to see you Libby. Alright? I'm no trying to be aw – I'm no a fucking charity case right, it's just this is my stuff here and I – I need this. Tae take action. Tae pay my way! Fuck!

Declan *punches himself in the head.*

Libby   Declan, stop it.

Declan   Fucking telling me how tay act! Still! What happens now then eh? Writer? You decide.

Libby   What do you want me to say, Declan? That you'll stick a knife in me? Come on!

Declan *turns the knife on himself and holds it against his neck.*

Declan   Naw, your first idea was better.

Libby   Declan.

Declan   Money. I need it. And it's fair. My story, my life. My money. Or this ends now.

Libby   Listen to me.

Beat.

I love you.

Declan *screams.*

Declan   Fuck! Off!

Projected text: Declan violently thrusts the knife across his neck

Declan, *still screaming, does not thrust the knife across his neck. A sharp change in the space, in light and sound.*

Scene Twenty-one

Libby   I scream. But I don't hear it. Or really notice that it's happening at all. Time is stretched out. Everything slows. And all I can see, under the lights, is Declan. He clutches his hand to his neck.

Projected text: Declan clutches his hand to his neck.

Declan *does not clutch his hand to his neck. He stands, staring at* **Libby**, *knife in his hand.*

He doubles over.

Projected text: He doubles over. He coughs. He splutters.

Projected text: He coughs. He splutters.

Declan   No.

Libby   He hacks at his wrists.

Projected text: He hacks at his wrists.

Declan   Naw, fuck you.

Libby   He falls to the ground.

Projected text: He falls to the ground.

Declan   That is not what happens, that is not how it happens.

Libby   Face down, Declan convulses and groans.

Projected text: Face down, Declan convulses and groans.

Declan   What happens is I run.

Libby   Declan holds his throat as blood spills from his body.

Projected text: Declan holds his throat as blood spills from his body.

Declan   I run.

Libby   It all looks very, very real.

Projected text: It all looks very, very real.

Declan   Back up the stairs, I run. Pushing past the lassie that works here. Pushing through the doors, through the bit with the tickets and the posters, running to get out. Out. Out ay this place, this fucking place.

Libby   And an ambulance is called.

Declan   And I hear a siren. And see blue lights.

Libby   And when they arrive, they arrive with police.

Declan   And I don't stop. I just keep running. And running.

Libby   And they put him in a stretcher and hook him up to a machine, and they handcuff him even though there's no point.

Declan   Charging past people at bus stops, outside pubs. And I dinnae even ken if I'm being chased anymair but I dinnae stop. Up the hill. Up the Crags. It's dark and there's naecunt here. My bit. Up here, my private bit, where I come. And I'm so outay breath that I want tae be sick. And I just stand there, wheezing.

Libby   All I see, is blood.

Delcan   Breathe. Breathe. You're okay. Just breathe.

Libby   His blood, on the stage, under the lights. Thick, dark, red. Like ink.

Declan   Wind, filling my lungs. Cold.

Libby   How the real stuff looks just like the fake stuff.

Declan   Breathe.

Libby   How you really could believe it was the same stuff, if you wanted to.

Declan   Looking out. At the town all lit up. All little lights. Twinkly. Like in a story book. I breathe in, the wind. Getting stronger. Like I can feel it pushing against my skin, my eyes, my teeth. Like it's trying to blow through me. Actually through me, as I drink it in, standing here looking out at it all. The Forth. Oot tay Leith, the Castle an that just like the postcards. And over in the distance, in the bit naebody looks at, I can see the flats at my bit. I can really see it aw fae up here. Each wee light, a different life. A kitchen window. A couple watching telly. Somebody putting their kid to bed. People arguing. Someone crying, someone laughing. All playing out at once in this same place, this same town, without even noticing that the other one exists. Without even seeing how you're all joined up. And I feel the tightening across my chest. Like drowning. Except it's mair like rising. Head-spinning, rising up, up, up.

I take oot Libby's pencils. And I throw them off the edge. Wee tiny bits of colour scattering across the rocks. And I take oot my pad, wi my drawings in. And open it on the first page, and tear that page out and hold it to the wind and let it go. It flies out of my hand. Like a bird. Or like a ghost. And maybe someone will find it and maybe they won't and I don't fucking care. I tear another page. And let it go. Another page. And let it go. Another page and let it go.

Everything is not alright. Everything is not alright. Everything is not alright. If everything is going to be alight then show me how.

Down below, I see blue flashing lights pulling in to the park. And I keep tearing the pages out. Pictures of Siân. The wee yin, out there, down there, somewhere. Somewhere. Fuck knows where, but somewhere eh.

Libby   I'm the writer. My job is to tell stories.

Declan   What happens next is up to me.

Libby   That's all that I can do.

Declan   What happens next is not for you.

Libby   And this is the final image.

Declan   Because there's never really an end, whatever happens. After you get up, and leave. And head back to your cars, or to the bus, or to the bar. Stories don't just end where you say they do. They keep on going and they're messy and they're real. And there is no final image. The last of my drawings flies away.

Blue flashing lights. They're coming. For me. And what happens next is –

What happens next is –

I stand. Looking out at my city. And I breathe. And what happens next is –

Declan & **Libby**   Blackout.

Blackout.

The Enemy

Kieran Hurley

Based on *An Enemy of the People* by Henrik Ibsen

The Enemy was first premiered by National Theatre of Scotland on 13 October 2021 at Dundee Rep before touring to The King's Theatre Edinburgh, Eden Court Inverness and Perth Theatre. Cast and creative team were as follows:

Creative Team

Writer: Kieran Hurley
Director: Finn den Hertog
Set and Costume Designer: Jen McGinley
Video Designer: Lewis den Hertog
Lighting Designer: Katharine Williams
Composer: Kathryn Joseph
Sound Designer: Matt Padden
Co-Movement Director: Vicki Manderson
Co-Movement Director: Robbie Gordon
Assistant Director: Leonie Rae Gasson
Casting Director: Laura Donnelly CDG
Original Set Design: Rosanna Vize

Performers

Hannah Donaldson	Kirsten Stockmann
Billy Mack	Derek Kilmartin
Neil McKinven	Benny Hovstad
Taqi Nazeer	Aly Aslaksen
Gabriel Quigley	Vonny Stockmann
Eléna Redmond	Petra Stockmann

Production Team

Production Manager: Alice Black
Lighting Supervisor: Amy Dawson
Stage Supervisor: Jock Dinsdale
Costume Supervisor: Sophie Ferguson
Deputy Stage Manager: Maddy Grant
Lighting Programmer: Ross Hunter
Costume Technician: Nicky McKean
Video Supervisor: Andy Reid

Assistant Stage Manager: Kat Siebert
Sound Supervisor: Andy Stuart
Company Stage Manager: Emma Yeomans

Access

Captioner: Glenda Carson
BSL Performance Interpreter: Amy Cheskin
Audio Describer: Emma-Jane McHenry

Scene One

Petra Stockmann *sits at home, duvet wrapped around her, eating a bowl of cereal. Her face is lit in cold blue laptop light.*

Projected video shows an archive montage of old industry, establishment shots of a now-dilapidated small town centre, a post-industrial west of Scotland coastline as corny music plays. Vox pops of present-day citizens of the town:

Citizen 1   To really understand this place, you've got to get to grips with the sheer scale of what was lost. You know? We used to have jobs here. Real jobs. And when that was taken away from us, well – everything else goes with it. Gone.

Citizen 2   The whole identity of the place. Our dignity. The place just gets forgotten about completely. The life expectancy is frightening, criminal really.

Citizen 3   A lot of folk don't stick here. Others maybe don't have a choice, maybe don't think about it much. It's just the way it is here. A shit hole.

Beat.

Citizen 3   I'm allowed to say that cos I'm from here, I hear you saying that and you're in trouble, haha!

Video cuts to **Aly***, walking the street, talking to the camera.*

Aly   As a musician and songwriter, I'm always fascinated by the different meanings of words. We all know that politicians are full of empty buzzwords. 'Innovation.' 'Growth.' 'Regeneration.' But what does it really mean? To regenerate? To bring new life. To be renewed, reformed, and reborn.

Cut to bright images of healthy people swimming, families on flumes, racquet sports, cycling through a forest, etc. Total change of vibe! A massive transformative redevelopment!

Aly   It's been a long time coming. And some said it would never happen. But the Big Splash resort will soon be opening its doors to visitors from all across the world! This amazing new holiday resort is a development on an unprecedented scale, combining a water theme park, an expansive health spa complex, an Olympic-standard swimming pool, leisure centre, cultural hub, and a world-leading state-of-the-art indoor beach compound!

Citizen 3   A beach resort! Here! Can you imagine. It's basically a total dream! A ridiculous dream!

Citizen 2   Not just rubbish jobs, like proper employment. Our young folk won't be forced to leave to find work. They're saying we'll actually have people coming *here*, for jobs and quality of life. The reversal is just. . . it's impossible to even put into words.

Citizen 4   Absolute least this town deserves –

Citizen 5   That's it. That's it.

Citizen 4   One hundred percent.

Citizen 5   We were saying that. It's like winning the World Cup. But God knows we deserve a change in our luck.

Citizen 6   The fact it was the two sisters as well, working to make it happen. A family from here. The story is just – proud. That's what I am. Just so proud of this place.

Citizen 1   Nobody actually thought this would happen! We've been waiting, hoping for years. Years! And it's finally come. It's our time, and we're raring to go! Bring it on! Ha ha! Cheers!

As this plays, action unfolds in various pockets of the stage. **Vonny Stockmann** *emerges, half-dressed. Full-politician garb from the waist up; pyjamas from the waist down.* **Benny Hovstad** – *stony-faced, tired – puts on his suit, does his tie in the mirror.* **Derek Kilmartin** *picks up an outsized teddy bear with a bow on it from somewhere and takes a photo of it on his phone.*

Onscreen, **Aly** *and* **Vonny** *stand among a crowd of townsfolk.*

Aly   It's going to cause a real –

Crowd   Big Splash!

Aly enters the stage space, filming himself on a handheld tripod or selfie stick. He moves effortlessly as he does so, the tech totally natural to him like an extra limb. He is a real pro at this.

Aly   I'm Aly Aslaksen, and I'll be running a series of bespoke events on all my platforms to coincide with the launch of the Big Splash resort, telling you all you need to know about this transformative development. Why? Because I'm a local boy who cares about the future of the place he came from – that's it. Follow me on Insta, Twitter and TikTok for ongoing updates on the opening of the resort and the bid to have the town named UK City of Regeneration. I'll be doing a set at our digital launch party, sponsored by Kilmartin Industries. So at me with suggestions for my crowd-sourced swimming-themed playlist.

Onstage, **Kirsten Stockmann** *enters, in the same room as* **Petra**.

Aly   Details are appearing on your screen right about now, so smash that like button, watch follow, share, and subscribe –

Kirsten *slaps the laptop shut, the video cuts out. She hurriedly sets about trying to get her stuff together, make* **Petra***'s lunch, and set up a tablet for a video call.*

Petra   Did you know that teenagers need to get on average around ten hours of sleep a night? And if we don't it can really have all sorts of negative effects.

Kirsten   Uh huh.

Petra   Headaches. Acne. *And* it can seriously impair our neurological functions. Like our ability to absorb information, to problem solve, and like even to just remember basic information like, names, and dates. And homework. So really, from a scientific perspective, forcing us to go into school at this time in the morning is actually not only oppressive but also has an adverse effect on the quality of our education.

Kirsten   It's nearly eight o'clock, Petra, get dressed.

Petra   It's just science. Just thought you'd be interested maybe in some of the scientific facts about what's going on for your daughter right now. Maybe that's why so many kids are off sick right now. Did you think of that?

Kirsten   Petra, I don't have the time for any of this, okay? Not today, so . . .

Petra   Ten hours, Mum! I don't get anything like that do I? I mean, just think of all the potential I must just be pissing away.

Kirsten   If you want to get more sleep, you can go to bed earlier. Simple.

Petra   Ah, I knew you'd say that. But here's a thing. It is *also* a scientific fact that biological sleep patterns shift towards a later time during adolescence, so it's natural for teenagers to not really be able to get to sleep at all until at least, like, eleven-thirty or whatever. And then that would be like not even waking up until half nine.

Kirsten   Well your mental arithmetic seems to be ticking over just fine for someone with seriously impaired neurological functions.

Petra   That's not even counting, like, if you're awake at night and can't sleep, cos you're thinking about stuff or you're anxious or whatever. Like, to really properly account for that I should definitely be staying in bed until at least noon.

Kirsten   Petra. What's the matter? Are you ill? You don't look ill.

Petra   If I say 'yes' will you let me stay at home, is that how this works?

Kirsten   You didn't drink the tap water did you?

Petra   You said it was probably fine.

Petra's *phone beeps. She looks at it. The message, projected, reads: 'Hiya weirdo. You gonna be at school today? Will see you later. Bitch.'*

Kirsten   It probably is fine.

Petra   Now that you've got a real job can you at least get me a decent phone? This is embarrassing.

Kirsten   What's the matter?

Petra   Nothing.

Kirsten   Look, I know it's not easy coming in to a new school. You just need to get out there and be yourself okay? It'll get easier.

Just stay true to yourself and the right people will come to you. When I was your age I wanted to go dogging off the whole time too, but –

Petra   What did you call it? Dogging?

Kirsten   Yes.

Petra   Ew.

Kirsten   What kind of mother would I be if I just let you stay off school whenever you felt like it?

Petra   A kind of. . . great one?

Kirsten *receives a video call.*

Kirsten   Back down here and dressed for school in *five minutes* okay? I've got to take this Skype call. It's your Auntie Vonny.

Petra   Skype? Literally nobody in the world uses Skype.

Kirsten   Your Auntie Vonny does. Now beat it.

The call connects. **Vonny** *appears onscreen. She remains visible in person elsewhere onstage.*

Vonny   Hello? Can you see me alright? Is it working? Now I don't have long –

Kirsten   I can hear you fine. Here we go eh! You excited?

Petra   Hi Auntie Vonny.

Vonny   Oh hiya honey!

Kirsten   Petra. Upstairs. Clothes on. Now.

Petra *sulkily drags herself off.*

Kirsten   She's trying to skive off. Again.

Vonny   How's she settling in, okay?

Kirsten   Ach, you know. Early days. She'll get there. She thinks the other kids single her out, for, you know. Being different.

Vonny   Well Kirsten hen, if you will give her a name like *Petra*, I mean –

Kirsten   You wanted to talk to me about the speech?

Vonny   Yes.

Kirsten   Can you not use a phone like a normal person?

Vonny   I'm keeping the line free, for a phoner with the BBC. Then I'm straight over for a livecast with your actual Aly Aslaksen!

Kirsten   Fancy. What's a livecast?

Vonny   I don't know. Have you written it yet?

Kirsten   Nearly.

Vonny   How near is nearly?

Kirsten   How soon is now, Vonny, Christ, I –

Vonny   Could you send me what you have just now? And then when you do finish, if you could send the finished one over too. Text me, so I can pick it up straight away –

Kirsten   I wasn't really planning on having anything typed up to be honest, I thought I'd just go with the flow.

Vonny   No. No, I told you, you need to have it written down so I can have it all properly checked. I can't have you just shooting from the hip Kirsten, I know what you're like.

Kirsten   People don't want a big speech, they want to celebrate! And you know I hate the whole public speaking thing. I'll just say that it's a privilege to be here, at this historic moment –

Vonny   Good. Good.

Vonny *turns her laptop so the webcam faces the wall, quickly finishes getting dressed.*

Kirsten   Some nice stuff about you for making this whole thing a reality –

Vonny   On that.

Vonny *turns the laptop back around and sits down.*

Vonny   I have some suggestions here about what you might try to cover.

Kirsten   You're kidding me on.

Vonny   You can hardly blame me for wanting to keep you on a tight leash, Kirst. This is the most important thing to happen to this town in any of our lifetimes. If you'd sent me your speech weeks ago like I asked you, I wouldn't have to do this.

Kirsten   I've just been a bit distracted alright, I've been busy. Sorry.

Vonny   On what like?

A knock. **Benny Hovstad** *enters, eating a pasty.*

Benny   Kirst! Oop. Sorry. I'm not interrupting am I?

Kirsten   My sister's just beamed herself into my kitchen to dictate my speech to me, it's fine.

Vonny   I am not dictating, I'm –

Benny   Morning Councillor.

Vonny   Provost, if you don't mind Benny.

Benny   Nae bother.

Vonny   I'm not dictating, Kirsten, I'm simply asking you to –

Kirsten   Send it to you to approve or rewrite it and make sure it says nice things about you?

Vonny   It's nothing personal. This is transformative for a lot of people, and they've been waiting a long time for it. We owe it to them, to get this right. We might be frontrunners for City of Regeneration but it's not in the bag yet, so –

Benny   Don't worry, Vonny, I'm sure you'll get the political recognition you deserve.

I mean no one's really bothered that it was your sister's idea in the first place –

Vonny   It was not Kirsten's idea! It was a tie! I mean – I mean, we came up with it together. That's what I mean. Benny what in God's name are you eating?

Benny   Steak bake.

Vonny   It's eight o'clock in the morning.

Benny   Correct.

Vonny   You'll be dead before sixty you know that?

Benny   Well. Better fill the remaining mornings with enjoyable breakfasts then.

Vonny   Kirsten you're a founding director of a bloody health centre, tell him.

Kirsten   She's not wrong, Benny.

Benny   Priorities but. Did you know that Greggs has a fully unionised workforce? Rarity these days. *And* they have an ever-increasing rate of pay, pegged to inflation. Wee factoid there. Don't get that at your Whole Foods do you? Ethical consumerism in action that's what this is. Up the workers!

Vonny   Not with my digestion. Look, I've got pressers all day, I've got to get on.

Kirsten   Don't let us stop you Vonny.

Vonny   Send me the speech alright?

Vonny *hangs up.*

Benny   Well she's nervous.

Kirsten   Not as nervous as me! Public speaking. Officialdom. Suits and ties and cameras. Gives me the creeps. Petra!

Benny   Do you want to practice on me? I can help.

Kirsten   Thanks, I'll be fine. Face your fears and that. I'll keep it short. Tell them the honest truth. That this is the proudest day of my life. That I never dreamed I'd see these plans become a reality. That it's no less than every one of the people here deserve, and it's a privilege just to be a part of it. Then I'll get out the way so folk can get to the bar!

Benny   You've done this before.

Kirsten *looks at her phone.*

Benny   City of Regeneration eh? Fuck me. They really do stretch the definition of 'city' with these things don't you think? Kirsten?

Kirsten   Hm?

Benny   Candy Crush is it?

Kirsten   What?

Benny   Your phone.

Kirsten   Oh – aye – no. I was just – I was expecting to hear from someone. Sorry. Tea?

Benny   Smashing, aye.

Benny *goes to make the tea.*

Kirsten   No! Sit down. Let me.

Benny *watches, slightly bemused as* **Kirsten** *fills the kettle up from a big bottle of water.*

Benny   Is everything alright Kirsten? You're – you're all – you're all fine here?

Kirsten   Yeah, I mean – it's more than I ever dreamed of, for Petra and me. A proper home, with a garden. Not like that damp shithole we were living in down there. You know I couldn't ever have imagined, when we were wee, that I'd wind up in one of these big houses. Petra's missing her old school and stuff, but she'll get there, you know how kids are.

Benny   Well, if there's anything you need –

Kirsten   I just need to start properly furnishing the place. Decorating. Lampshades. Things like that. That's what folk do, I think.

Benny   I was just checking you're okay – for money and everything –

Kirsten   I'm fine. I'm finally earning something now. We're fine. Really. Thanks though.

Benny   Good good. Life gets easier when you sell out to the man eh?

Kirsten   Hey watch it you. I like to think of it more like growing up, thank you very much. Making actual change, in the real world.

Benny   Absolutely.

Kirsten   I'm not saying we've not had to make some uncomfortable compromises, but that's just –

Benny   I'm yanking your chain, the whole thing is fucking brilliant you know that.

Kirsten   I do.

Benny   You're still giving me my interview later aye?

Kirsten   Course!

Benny   Tremendous. Dr Kirsten Stockmann, the wild child! The prodigal daughter coming home to usher in a bright new dawn!

Kirsten   You can't call me that.

Benny   What?

Kirsten   I'm not a doctor, you know that!

Benny   Ach, nobody cares about stuff like that!

Kirsten   I do. It's the truth.

Benny   It's the story that counts! A big triumphant homecoming, people love that. Come on! Yes!

Benny grabs **Kirsten** *and gives her a twirl.* **Kirsten** *laughs.*

Benny   There we go!

Kirsten   You're ridiculous you know that?

Benny   'Scuse me?

Kirsten   You're a ridiculous person.

Benny   I've been called worse. How's Petra?

Kirsten   Is it a stupid name?

Benny   Sorry?

Kirsten   Petra's not a stupid name is it? Is Petra a stupid name?

Benny   Not at all, it's lovely. How?

Kirsten   It's a strong name. It means rock. It's strong.

Petra *enters, wearing her school uniform.*

Petra   It means 'Peter' actually, and yes it is stupid.

Benny   Petra! There she is! How are you darling?

Petra   What's he doing here?

Kirsten   Petra don't be so rude. Here you are Benny.

Benny   Ta, love. Just popping in to say hi, check in on your mum ahead of tonight. You'll be the toast of the school today I should have thought.

Petra   Doubt it. They all hate me. I hate it there.

Kirsten   Petra.

Benny   Ha. Good attitude. I was the same. Hated it. All that keeping your head down, not stepping out of line, regurgitating the same old bollocks. You're a smart girl, Petra. Bet you're a right thorn in the side of those teachers. Am I right?

Petra   Mum.

Benny   The important thing is to be an *independent thinker*, that's what they don't teach you. That's the one thing they don't want you to learn, the hypocrites.

Petra *looks at* **Benny***, openly unimpressed.*

Benny   I only had one teacher I liked. There's always one, I think. Mine was Mr McDonald. History. The rest of the teachers hated him. He was all about teaching young folk to speak truth to power. A romantic old sod maybe, but he meant it. He's the reason I got into journalism, I think. Who's your favourite teacher Petra?

Petra   Dunno. Ms Quinn. Media Studies.

Benny   Media Studies eh? Fantastic. We never got anything like that. Ms Quinn. She's a real inspiration then is she?

Petra   No. She's a supply teacher. She just puts on old films and sits and does the sudoku. I've seen the first forty-five minutes of *Grease*, the first forty-five minutes of *Indiana Jones: Raiders of the Lost Ark*, and the first forty-five minutes of *Labyrinth* with David Bowie. Might watch the second half of that one day actually, I'd quite like to find out what happens to the baby.

Kirsten   Here.

Petra   What's this?

Kirsten   Packed lunch, what's it look like. Benny, let yourself out we have to dash.

Petra   Why are we still doing packed lunches? Bet it's something weird.

Kirsten   I'm not suddenly made of cash Petra. It's not weird, it's a hummus sandwich.

Here, take another one of these.

Petra   A *hummus sandwich*? You do know that's the kind of thing that'll get me my cunt kicked in don't you?

Kirsten   Petra! Jesus!

Petra   What? That's just how they talk here! You're the one that said I had to make an effort to try to fit in!

Kirsten   Just get in the fucking car, will you?

Petra   Nice trousers by the way.

Petra *takes the bottle of water, and exits.*

Kirsten   Is there something wrong with my trousers? What's wrong with my trousers?

Benny   Nothing. They look. . . magnificent.

Kirsten   These are my best trousers.

Benny   Well it's a day that befits the wearing of one's best trousers.

Kirsten   Exactly.

Benny   I'll see you later aye?

Kirsten   You will. Here.

Kirsten *leaves, tossing house keys to* **Benny**, *who catches them. Alone,* **Benny** *picks up the open water bottle, sniffs its contents, thinks, drinks his tea.*

Scene Two

Kirsten*'s car. It is chucking it outside.*

Petra   He *is* a creep, Mum, he is such a creep. He is absolutely king of the creeps.

Kirsten   Oh, stop it.

Petra   If he was a famous actor he'd be Meryl Creep.

Kirsten   Benny is an old family friend, and a sweetheart. And he's been a big help getting us settled in, you know that.

Petra   If he was a small French restaurant he would be Un Creeperie.

Kirsten   Petra.

Petra   If he was a Radiohead song he'd be 'Fake Plastic Creeps'.

Kirsten   Enough.

Silence. **Petra** *looks at her phone.*

Kirsten   You'll let me know if there's more off sick today will you?

Petra   Yes.

Kirsten   How many is it now? Eight? Nine?

Petra   Twelve yesterday.

Kirsten   Twelve?

Petra's *phone vibrates.*

Kirsten   Is that me? Is that – Petra will you pass me my phone please?

Petra   It's mine.

The text message on **Petra**'s *phone reads Grandad: Gonnae tell your mum I said hi? Joke.*

Kirsten   Oh. Right.

Grandad: But serisly. Tell her Im rooting for her and hope launch goes well.

Kirsten   Is that you or –

Petra   Mum, they're all me. Will you chill out.

Kirsten   I'm expecting someone. Who's texting you so much?

Petra   Grandad.

Kirsten   I do wish you wouldn't call him that. He's not your grandad.

Petra   He's my dad's dad isn't he? He says to tell you he hopes it goes well tonight. And that he's rooting for you.

Kirsten   He doesn't mean that. What does he want?

Petra   Nothing.

Kirsten   Derek Kilmartin never wants nothing Petra, what does he want?

Petra   Nothing! We're just chatting.

Petra *texts:*

I told her. She says go fuck yourself, basically.

Grandad: lol course she does

Grandad: Have you been to Gio's yet? Smashing ice cream. Let's meet there.

Petra   He's gonna take me to the ice cream shop at lunchtime. Aw. Cute.

Grandad: [Ice cream emoji. Sunglasses emoji.]

Petra   Why do you hate him so much?

Kirsten   Can't you just, hang out with your own friends or something.

Petra   Back in London you mean?

Kirsten   Sorry. I'm just, nervous. Alright? A big day.

The car stops. **Petra** *goes to get out.*

Kirsten   'Creep', by the way. You could have just said 'Creep'.

Petra   What?

Kirsten   Radiohead already have a song called 'Creep'. It would have worked better if you'd just said 'Creep'.

Petra   Oh. Well I don't know do I, what am I like fifty?

A phone buzzes.

Petra   That one was you.

Petra *leaves.* **Kirsten** *fumbles for her phone. She sees the message. We see flashes of the subject line on screen, the following words briefly visible: 'URGENT.' 'Tests positive.' 'Contamination.' 'Water.'*

Kirsten   No. No, no, no. No.

Scene Three

Vonny *is filming a livecast interview with* **Aly**, *onstage and projected. Elsewhere onstage throughout,* **Kirsten** *watches the interview between* **Vonny** *and* **Aly**, *visibly anxious. She paces. Reads. Sinks her face into her hands. Freaks the fuck out.*

Aly   Vonny, you know I gotta say, in the run-up to this a lot of people were saying to me, 'Aly, it's not really like you to get a straight-laced politician on the show. . .'

Vonny   Careful who you're calling 'straight-laced' wee man!

Aly   And that's what I told them! Because you're like me, we both grew up here –

Vonny   Right, yeah.

Aly   And like me, you'll have seen first-hand how the people of this town have been ignored, right? Cast aside by governments –

Vonny   Oh aye, for decades Aly. I was at primary school here in the eighties, and I remember it well – I've seen that legacy of repeated failed promises, and the effect that has had.

Aly   It has to be said, not everyone was delighted about the plans at first. There's been a lot of suspicion, of big developments with big promises, and not without reason either.

Vonny   Of course, and there's always going to be people who want to stoke those sorts of fears, for their own political ends. And so when we looked at the benefits, on health, jobs, tourism – but more than that, on people's *lives* Aly – I just knew it had to happen. And I think people really do see that.

Aly   It's a big deal, it must have been a tough gig getting it over the line.

Vonny   It wasn't always easy, no, but it was a matter of political will. It took imagination and effort. Combing private investment with public funds, pulling it all together by hook or by crook. That's the true spirit of this town, I think. Knowing that sometimes you have to roll up your sleeves and get on with it. And now, tonight's launch event also sees shares floated in the resort for the first time, which we hope will be the start of new investment, new money coming into the town. But we're also inviting you, the citizens of the town, to become shareholders yourselves through our 'Be Big Splash' community buy-in programme – so don't miss out. Aly, delivering the Big Splash Resort is what we promised to do, it's what we were elected to do, and I'm extremely proud to say: it's what we've done.

Aly   That right there is what I'm talking about. Provost, yes.

Thank you.

And you can look forward to hearing much, much more from Vonny Stockmann and her sister Kirsten at the Big Splash resort later tonight as we launch our bid for UK City of Regeneration. Meantime you can find out more about Be Big Splash by following the hashtag #BeBigSplash, and why don't you lovely people get in touch with your own memories of growing up here, or your hopes for our future? Tell us what excites you most about Big Splash. Vonny thanks a million for joining us yeah?

Vonny   Thank you. Uh, party on!

Kirsten *switches the interview off. She takes a deep breath. She decides. She leaves.*

Scene Four

Benny Hovstad*'s office. He is sitting idly at his desk, picking unhappily at a salad. He is watching nonsense on the internet. Like* *a video of a comically bad penalty kick, or someone falling in a lake, or maybe someone doing a tutorial on some ludicrous kitchen hack on TikTok. There is a knock at the door.*

Benny *closes YouTube and opens a live graph of the FTSE 100 as* **Kirsten** *enters.*

Benny   Kirst. You're early.

Beat.

Kirsten   Your receptionist wasn't there, I just thought I'd –

Benny   Is everything okay, Kirst, you look like someone's died.

Beat.

Benny   Has someone died?

Kirsten   She's sick is she? Your receptionist?

Benny   What? Aye, aye, dinnae worry about –

Kirsten   She been off long?

Benny   Few days.

Kirsten   Anyone else off sick?

Benny   Um. We've had one or two maybe. Change of weather, like.

Kirsten   There's been twelve kids ill in Petra's class.

Benny   Something going round, I suppose. It happens you know, we never used to make such a big fuss out of it.

Kirsten   Vomiting bile. Nausea. Diarrhoea. A burning in the stomach is what they're saying, like their insides are on fire. Must be over one hundred and fifty off across the whole school.

Benny   What's this about hen? Is Petra okay?

Kirsten   Journalists hear things off the record, right Benny?

Benny   Uh huh?

Kirsten   Like there's a code of practice and everything, so that if I say 'this is off the record' you sort of have to agree. Right?

Benny   Um. Aye, something like that.

Kirsten   And we're friends right?

Benny   For sure.

Beat.

Kirsten   They've been drinking poison. The kids. Your receptionist. Everyone, actually. The water in the town it's, it's, it's toxic. All of it. And we did it. We've poisoned them, Benny. The whole town. Actual poison.

Benny   What?

Beat.

Kirsten   When they were building the resort. They, they rerouted the, the pipes. The town's water infrastructure. The plumbing and stuff. To be able to supply the new development with, with enough, with the, with the –

Benny   Water?

Kirsten   Water. Yes. To get the necessary water supply. For a massive development like this. They were worried that it was holding the thing up okay? But Vonny wanted everything completed on schedule so that we'd be in time to make the bid. For City of, City of, City of –

Benny   City of Regeneration.

Kirsten   City of fucking Regeneration. And I warned them. I tried to warn them and – they rushed it through anyway.

Benny   Rushed what through?

Kirsten   The plumbing. They cut corners, somehow, I don't know. To get it finished on time. And now the water supply is letting in a, a – well it's a toxicity. A contamination.

Benny   Right.

Kirsten   Into the whole town. And that's why your receptionist is off sick. That's why the school is full of empty chairs. And there's only going to be more. I honestly don't know how bad it gets. But I know it's there.

Pause.

Benny   Jesus.

Beat.

Benny   How do you know this?

Kirsten   I had a few samples sent to a lab.

Benny   Samples of what?

Kirsten   Tap water. From my house. And from random spots, across town. One from here actually. And from the Resort. It's contaminated. All of it. And all in the same way.

Benny   And you never thought to mention it before now?

Kirsten   I didn't know anything before now! It was a hunch! I tried to put it out my mind, told myself I was just taking precautions. I expected to hear back weeks ago! I didn't want to set off the alarm without knowing, did I? You know exactly how that story goes. 'Here's Kirsten, stirring up bother again!' You know what my sister's like, she'd never have listened!

Benny   But you cannae like – the water looks fine. It tastes fine. Smells fine. You cannae see it or that.

Kirsten   No Benny you can't bloody see it!

Benny   Well where's it coming from? The – the fucking – contamination. The poison.

Kirsten   I can't prove that yet but it seems obvious doesn't it? Think of the nearest literal cesspit.

Pause.

Benny   Derek Kilmartin's land. The dump.

Kirsten *nods.*

Benny   Oh ya fucker. Well. This is awkward for yous.

Kirsten   Petra is seeing him today. She insists on calling him 'grandad.'

Benny   Eesh. And you're sure – like absolutely sure – that the water's –

Kirsten   One hundred percent.

Benny   When did you get the tests back?

Kirsten   Today. Got the email this morning. After I saw you.

Benny   And what did it say?

Kirsten   That it's fucked. The water's fucked. We're fucked.

Silence.

Benny   Wow.

Pause.

Benny   What do we about the resort? I mean people are, people are expecting that – I mean it can't. It can't now. It's gonna have to – they can't open now can they? They'll have to shut it down?

Beat.

Benny   Oh shite.

Kirsten   I don't know how we're going to tell them.

Silence. **Kirsten** *stares at* **Benny***, desperate.*

Benny   Here. Look. Right. Okay. Right. Look. At least we know now right? I mean really, to know and do something about it, than not know at all. You've done brilliantly here Kirst, actually. This, look, this is good. This is good. Think about it. If you hadn't found this out this could have been even worse, like, really really bad –

Kirsten   Yes. Aye. Disastrous.

Benny   Well, you've just saved the day, Kirsten! Thank God you're here, or we'd all be even more screwed. You've said lives, probably –

Kirsten   I need to tell Vonny, it'll crush her –

Benny Crush her! She's gonna kiss you! You've just rescued her political career! Imagine she'd gone and cracked on with the whole thing, not knowing this. She'd be toast. Fuck, she'll probably try to make out the whole thing was her discovery!

Kirsten You don't think people will be furious? They will, they'll be fucking furious!

Benny Aye maybe, but they're always furious! And anyway, only if it's put to them the wrong way. Was it Vonny's fault that Kilmartin's been letting his corporate mates dump their shite around the town while everyone turns a blind eye? No. It's the fault of the, I dunno, government, probably. Or even better, the previous council. Isn't it?

Kirsten Yeah, but that's not really –

Benny Something has to be done! Right? As soon everyone understands that this is a crisis averted, they'll be over the moon with relief! Wouldn't you?

Kirsten And if it, if it all falls through, the resort, my job and everything I mean, then . . .

Benny It won't! They'll figure all that out. Temporary repairs. You're gonna be a local hero doll. 'There goes the lassie that saved us all from drinking Kilmartin's toxic death juice!' You'll never have to buy a drink in this town again Kirsten, this is huge.

Kirsten Right, well, I mean –

Benny Yes! Come on! This is great. We'll help. We'll run a big piece on it for you, get the word out –

Kirsten I was speaking off the record, Benny.

Benny Of course! And I would never – you know that. But we're gonna have to act fast. And people are gonna have to know aren't they?

Kirsten Yes, they are.

Benny Well then. You just say the word. The sooner the better, so we can seize control of the story. Proper investigative journalism for a change, a big scoop. Real light in the darkness stuff, like the old days man. Yes! It should be in your words though. Can you get something to me by this afternoon?

Kirsten   Well – yes, right aye. Thank you, Benny. Thank you. I'll be in touch. Thank you!

Benny   You're a hero, Kirsten. A hero!

Scene Five

A cafe. **Petra** *sits with* **Derek***, next to the teddy bear and a Knickerbocker Glory the size of a small house.*

Derek   The truth is Petra, I've always liked your mother. I have. She was always a trouble maker even when she was much younger, you know that? Getting involved in her protests and all that business. Did she ever tell you about the time she organised a school walk-out against the Iraq war?

Petra *shakes her head.*

Derek   She must've been about your age. The teachers got wind of it a few days before, threatened everyone with a month's worth of lunchtime detentions. So when your mum heard that everyone else had bottled it and nobody was gonna join her, she just went into school early that day. Chained herself to the gates with a bike lock so no one could get in. School was shut the whole day, they had to get in the fire brigade to cut her loose!

Petra *chuckles.*

Derek   Aye, she didn't take nonsense from anyone. Can't say I always agreed with her *beliefs* and everything but she had spunk. I admired that. I think that's what my Andy liked about her too.

Petra   I wish I could have met him.

Derek   I wish you could have too. Sometimes. But then I remember what an awful prick he was and I think well, maybe it's best you never. Course I tried to help your mum after she took you

down south. Offered her money and stuff. She tell you that? Thought
not. She wouldn't take it. Said it was dirty money, coming from a
dirty great big businessman like me. She had all her environmental
principles and things. Then she had all the legal fees from the
protests and that, still wouldnae take it so she had to work twice as
hard –

Petra   She's a fucking idiot!

Derek   Well, I'm glad you're back. I know you're too old for
teddy bears and stuff, I just – want to make up for all the lost years
of buying you nice things. You're here now. Time to make things
right. Here, your tea's getting cold.

Petra   Oh – I can't have it, sorry.

Derek   Why's that?

Petra   Mum won't let me. Made me promise.

Derek   It's fairtrade, probably. They're all fairtrade these days.

Petra   No it's – she's made me promise not to drink the tap
water.

Derek   Eh? The water here is magic. Much better than the waxy,
chalky, lukewarm London piss you're used to. Tastes lovely and
crisp and freezing right out the tap.

Petra   She says it's making everyone sick.

Derek   Really?

Petra   I think it's part of her ongoing mission to make sure
everyone at school singles me out as a little weirdo. Sometimes
think if my dad was here I'd fit in more.

Derek   It's just your accent love, that's all.

Petra   Cheers, Grandad.

Derek   They'll get over it once they get to know you. It's just
they think it puts you up here you know? With them down there.
And they hate that.

Petra   I'm not posh.

Derek   That's just not how they see it though. And if there's one thing folk in this town can't stand it's when they think someone's acting like they're above them. Because people here hate success. It's a sickness they have, a kind of jealousy. Unless you're doing an Aly Arselicker, some pop star or whatever he is doing some charity drive, on the internet, prancing like a tit. They love that. Here, eat your ice cream. You've not touched it.

Petra   It's the campest thing I've ever seen in my life, look at it. I'm scared to touch it, in case it breaks into song.

Derek   That's a proper Knickerbocker Glory love, that's what that is. Homemade Scottish Italian ice cream made by the same family for four generations. You don't get that in your bloody Shoreditch, do you?

Petra   Mm. It's really good.

Derek   Told you.

Petra   Have some.

Derek   No, it's yours, it's for you, it's a present.

Petra   I can't eat all of this I'll be sick, here.

Derek   Oh go on then. Oh, fucking hell. 'Scuse me.

They both laugh as **Derek** *tries to eat a bigger scoop of ice cream than his tiny spoon can manage.*

Derek   Bloody hell that's good. Here.

Derek *helps himself to some more.* **Petra** *laughs.*

Derek   So here, tell me about this tap water thing?

Scene Six

Kirsten *sits at home, typing at her laptop. She is on the phone, to* **Benny** *who sits elsewhere onstage with* **Aly**.

Kirsten Aye, I'm nearly finished. I couldn't get through to Vonny. Sent her an email. She text to say she's coming round, she's on her way over now.

Benny Just a text? Weird. She'll be buying time to think about how she can take the credit for saving the day no doubt.

Kirsten Probably. I don't mind to be honest. I think it's pretty good what I've got here, it might be a bit over-long and a bit heavy on the sort of science speech –

Benny Don't worry about that. I can help with all of that. Just get me the bloody thing. Here, there's someone I want you to meet.

Kirsten Who? Who?

Benny Only one Aly Aslaksen, he's raring to say hi –

Kirsten Benny fucking hell, we said off the record, no one else is supposed to know yet, Vonny's not even –

Benny It's cool, it's cool, it is off the record. I'm just, you know, getting our ducks in a row for when we make the big splash – uh, no pun intended – here – someone wants to say hello –

Aly Hiya there Kirsten.

Kirsten Oh, hi –

Aly Benny's given me the whole scoop. It's really fucking bad right?

Kirsten I'm afraid so. I'm so sorry.

Aly No, no. It's – it's good you've found this out. Because now we can start to turn this oil tanker around right?

Kirsten Yes, exactly, it's quite urgent.

Aly Well, as I've said to Benny already, I'm very happy to help. I know I'm just some podcast guy, I'm not a scientist or anything like you, but I do have a bit of a following in these parts. You know, I saw this documentary about Flint, Michigan? If we wanted to do some high profile awareness raising shit –

Kirsten   I don't think any of that will be necessary yet.

Aly   Oh of course, I'm just spit-balling ideas you know –

Kirsten   What about the launch tonight?

Aly   Yeah. Talk to your sister. Let's find out. If we cancel we cancel, obviously. I mean no one's gonna pretend it's not a ballache, but needs must. I think that once everyone's up to speed then maybe it's okay. We could use the launch as a ready-made platform, to let people know. People of the town all there, people tuned in online, gathered press –

Kirsten   Okay. Okay. Great.

Aly   You're gonna need to re-write your speech though! You're the main event now Kirsten. The hero, Benny tells me. 'We could be heroes, just for one day!' Ha. Except, longer, because you're gonna make a really lasting impact on people's general wellbeing and so forth. Listen I have to dash, I've got my Twitch stream coming up –

Kirsten   Not a word of this okay, please don't mention –

Aly   Lips. Sealed. Awaiting further instructions Commander. If there's anything I can do to help, I've got your number from Benny here I'm gonna text you mine alright. Be in touch. We're all behind you in this. The whole town *will* be behind you on this. I promise.

Kirsten   Thank you. Thank you, Aly. I really appreciate your help. It means a lot.

Aly   Ha ha, no problemo Kirsten. Ciao.

Benny   See you Aly.

Aly   Ta ta Benzo.

Aly *leaves.*

Benny   You still there?

Kirsten   You weren't meant to tell anyone. Benzo.

Benny   Och, come on. Aly's not gonna go rogue with this. He's a
fanny. All hot air and wish trees, following around his trendy causes
like he's fucking Bono. But, people here genuinely listen to him.

Kirsten   It was nice of him to say 'the whole town is behind you.'
That was very sweet.

Benny   Alright Mrs 'I had your poster on my wall' keep your
knickers on. The whole town will be behind you! You can count on
us. Okay?

A knock at the door.

Kirsten   That's her.

It's not locked Vonny, come in.

Derek *enters. Face mask around his chin, perhaps.*

Kirsten   Benny I've got to go.

Kirsten *hangs up. She looks up. She sees* **Derek**.

Kirsten   What do you want?

Derek   No need to be rude. I won't stay long, don't worry. Is it
true?

Kirsten   Is what true?

Derek   This moonshine of yours about wee beasties living in the
taps.

Kirsten   Sorry? Who have you been speaking to?

Derek   Petra. She says you won't let her drink the tap water.
Don't be angry at her, she was just trying to look after her
grandfather.

Kirsten   I don't know what you're talking about.

Derek   The tap water here is magic. You know that. She says
you're worried it's making people sick.

Kirsten   You know something, I would appreciate if you would
give her a bit of space. I don't like how you're crowding her out,
she's –

Derek   I'm just trying to make her feel welcome.

Kirsten   You can't just buy your way into this family all of a sudden, I made that very, very clear –

Derek   Of course.

Beat.

Derek   So, wee beasties in the water is it? Brilliant.

Kirsten   I don't know what you're talking about –

Derek   What, like cockroaches or something aye? Living in the plumbing! I know me and you have never seen eye to eye, but these wee beasties of yours wouldn't have anything to do with the fact I've got quite a lot invested in this resort would they?

Kirsten   Not beasties. Toxins. And no, that's a ludicrous thing to say.

Derek   Toxins. Right. And it's just you that can see them is it? Using, what, science? And magic woo-woo?

Kirsten   No. Nobody can see it. It's a microscopic contamination, it's – nobody can see it, that doesn't mean it's not there –

Derek   Nobody can see it but that doesn't mean it's not there! Like God. Or a fart! And you know where they're coming from do you? You know how they got in there, these magic beasties?

Beat.

Kirsten   Not yet.

Beat.

Derek   Okay then.

Beat.

Derek   Listen, I don't know why you're doing this but if you think it will embarrass your sister, or send me up and hurt me in some way then it's a bit of a kamikaze way of going about it –

Kirsten   None of this is fun for me, Derek, but it's real. And I will prove to you that it's real –

Vonny *enters.*

Derek   Well don't let me stand in your way. Oh. Hiya Vonny.

Vonny   Mr Kilmartin,

Derek   Right. I was on my way anyway. Cheerio lassies.

Wee beasties! Ha!

Derek *leaves.*

Vonny   What's he talking about?

Kirsten   Nothing. Petra's been seeing a lot of him. I was asking him to back off. That's all.

Vonny   Right.

Beat.

Vonny   I got your email.

Kirsten   You've read it I take it?

Vonny   Oh aye. Aye.

Kirsten   Don't worry I'm not gonna do a whole 'I told you so' thing, let's just start where we are and work on fixing this. I think we have to count ourselves lucky that we found out when we did, before it gets much worse –

Vonny   I mean it's not *wonderful* timing. It's not like we had anything planned for later on this evening or that.

Kirsten   I only got the test results today. I know, that is a bit of a nightmare obviously.

Vonny   Was it really necessary? For you to go making these wee investigations behind my back?

Kirsten   It was just speculative. Precautionary. I didn't want to say anything until I was certain, I knew how much you wanted me not to rock the boat and *disrupt things*.

Vonny   And you're certain now then?

Kirsten   Oh, absolutely.

Vonny   Right. And, I'm imagining you're going to want to take this to the board, and to the council. In some kind of official form?

Kirsten   Yes, of course.

Vonny   In your email you use some, pretty colourful language. 'An uninterrupted and unending stream of poison into the whole town.' It's, well it's –

Kirsten   It's what it is. Whether you drink it, swim in it, sit in a bloody steam room with it, that's what it is.

Vonny   And your solution would be, what? To shut down the whole water supply? And re-route the plumbing serving the entire town?

Kirsten   Unless you've a better idea? And we'll need to issue some kind of cease and desist notice to Kilmartin too, and quickly. Stop him letting out his land for dumping industrial waste. It's criminal –

Vonny   'We'll' need to issue a cease and desist?

Kirsten   You. You will.

Vonny   I don't like Kilmartin any more than you do but that's a licensed waste disposal plant he runs –

Kirsten   You're having me on, Vonny.

Vonny   I don't have the authority to just go around shutting down businesses with impunity, Kirsten, I'm a local councillor I'm not bloody Mugabe. Now this, this, plumbing work you propose. The water providers will have their own view on that I imagine, but you're aware that even the workaround is likely to cost a few quid, yes?

Kirsten   I'm not a wee kid, Vonny, of course 'I'm aware' of that.

Vonny   Like, a few million quid.

Kirsten   Well, we have to find the money from somewhere then.

Vonny   'We' again, is it?

Kirsten   You. You do.

Vonny   Right.

Kirsten   I can help. I'm sure people will want to help.

Vonny   Great. Like how?

Kirsten   Crowdfunding. I dunno, I've not really –

Vonny   The compensation to local business, the bureaucracy processing all of that – that costs money. Daily deliveries of bottled water to every home, every business. Running that operation, that's a cost. A massive one. Is that coming from the same GoFundMe page or is that separate?

Kirsten   It'd only be temporary. And it just has to be done. Political will and all that.

Vonny   We don't have any money, Kirsten.

Kirsten   Then, the government will have to step in.

Vonny   Sure, aye. I'll just ring them up. Off the back of what, some tests run in your mate's lab on the fly? That'll do it.

Kirsten   You can commission a fuller investigation, obviously if that's what you need but you need to turn the taps off first because we already know that it's poison –

Vonny   Turn the taps off. Cute. And do you know how long it'll take? To 'turn the taps off' and install an alternative water infrastructure, in this manner you suggest?

Kirsten   No. A long time. Obviously.

Vonny   About two years I should have thought, all in. Maybe three. That's if it all goes without a snag. And what do we do with the Resort in that time, eh?

Kirsten   Well we'd have to shut it, obviously.

Vonny   Obviously.

Kirsten   It would only be temporary –

Vonny   And do you suppose anybody would want to come to the place after we re-opened? What sort of advertising campaign do you imagine I might run in order to entice tourists to this, our supposedly life-giving health spa, once the town's reputation as an unbearable toxic shit hole has been fully established in the national press?

Kirsten   But that's what it is, Vonny, those are just the facts –

Vonny   And at this juncture too? On the day we're about to launch an extremely expensive bid in a nationwide competition to recognise us as the best regeneration project in the fucking country? When I've been busting a gut in the press to get the message out that this town is open for business, and when people have been sitting up and taking notice of the fact that we even *exist* for the first time since the seventies! Honestly, Kirsten. I knew that bringing you up here was a risk. That you might use your position to do something stupid and destructive. But I didn't quite imagine it would be on such a fucking existential scale. This is something, this really is quite something even for you.

Kirsten   This isn't about me, it's about the whole town.

Vonny   It is precisely and only because of the resort that this town has any future worth talking about, and you know that.

Kirsten   People are getting extremely sick right now, Vonny, as we speak. There are kids, children who are –

Vonny   I'm not convinced the matter is as serious as you've made it out to be.

Kirsten   As serious! If anything it's worse! They're only ill for now, but when they start dying, Vonny, what then?

Vonny   I don't think you have sufficient proof for such a massive undertaking.

Kirsten   I have proof that the water is toxic. And people. Are. Already. Sick.

Vonny   Do you even have any idea of the absolute litany of health problems that plague a community like ours, all the time?

Do you have any idea what decades of neglect does to the health of a place like this? The people round here have been shat on, *forever*, and I for one remain committed to turning that around. Some of us actually stuck around here, and we don't need your outlandish theories. These people aren't sick because they're poisoned, Kirsten. They're sick because they're poor.

Kirsten   You're being astonishingly irresponsible.

Vonny   No. No. I'm doing the only responsible thing. In light of all factors. All variables. We open the resort as planned. There is too much at stake, and not enough evidence to justify changing course at this stage. We tell nobody about this – for now. I will of course, as you say, commission some further investigations into what you think you've discovered here. I will raise it with the board of the resort, privately, when the time is right. But until then not a word of this gets out to anyone else –

Kirsten   Bit late for that I'm afraid, sorry.

Vonny   Who? Kirsten, who? No. Not Benny fucking Hovstad Kirsten, come on.

Kirsten   Fraid so. And boy is he keen. All that chest-thumping, greater purpose stuff. It's got him fired right up so it has.

Vonny   You went straight to the fucking press, before you even told *me* –

Kirsten   I spoke to him as friend. It is off the record –

Vonny   Christ you've really absolutely no idea how any of this works do you?

Beat.

Vonny   And you never even think of the damage all this could do to yourself? Eh?

Kirsten   At least I understand there are more important things than my own reputation –

Vonny   Well la-di-fucking-da. I think you're in danger of forgetting what side your bread is buttered on here. Was it not me that sent money to help you when you were putting yourself through university *pursuing your dreams*? Do you think I would have been able to afford to do *any* of that without having spent my life maintaining the integrity of my professional reputation?

Kirsten I'm grateful for all that but this is bigger than –

Vonny And now you want to talk to me about 'looking after my reputation' as if that is somehow a dirty, shitey thing to do? Grow up! Who do you think made sure you got this bloody job in the first place?

Kirsten I got the job on merit, the resort was my idea, it was outlined in my PhD thesis –

Vonny Failed PhD thesis. You know what I think, I think you got bored. I think things were looking too settled for you so you had to kick shite around the place to create a bit of drama –

Kirsten Oh fuck off. You can't just sit on something like this, you're going to have to deal with it sooner or –

Vonny I want you to prepare a full retraction, to be published in the event that questions start to be asked.

Kirsten What?

Vonny Now you've let the word out, we've got to be prepared. You'll say the situation is not as critical as you once feared, and that there is no cause for alarm.

Kirsten Vonny, listen. I deal in public health okay, I can't just – I have a right, in a free society to speak my mind. And people have a basic right to know the truth –

Vonny Wind your fucking neck in, Kirsten! This is my job. Putting out fires like this is what I do, and I'm good at it. And I really don't want this to have to get ugly sis, I really, really don't.

Kirsten You've made up your mind about this then?

Vonny I don't believe there is sufficient evidence for such a drastic course of action.

Kirsten   Okay. Fine.

Vonny   We'll look into this, privately, and within a reasonable budget.

Kirsten   Right.

Vonny   And in the meantime, we're pressing on with things as they are. Send me your speech as soon it's done, okay?

Kirsten   Okay.

Vonny   Okay. Good. It's good you're so principled, Kirsten. There's just proper ways of going about things that's all. Just leave that stuff to me, alright? You'll get there.

Kirsten   Got it.

Vonny   Okay. No hard feelings. A big day ahead, we all need to be on the same team.

Kirsten   What's next for you today then?

Vonny   Committee meeting. Then more interviews. Then over to the resort for a site visit before tonight –

Kirsten   Busy.

Vonny   Aye.

Kirsten   Let me fix you a cup of tea –

Vonny   No, no thanks, I have to be off –

Kirsten   A cold drink then – won't take a second. Here.

Kirsten *pours a full pint of water from the tap. She sets it down in front of* **Vonny**.

Kirsten   You have to stay hydrated, Vonny. Can't have you getting a headache.

Beat.

Kirsten   Come on, drink it.

Vonny   Kirsten.

Kirsten   What? If it's fine it's fine, isn't it? Thirsty, tiring work this, serving the people. So better drink up.

Vonny   I don't have to play this childish wee game.

Kirsten   Drink it.

Pause.

Vonny   I'm not thirsty.

Kirsten   Right. I'll add that to my statement will I? 'The situation is not as critical as I once feared and there is no cause for alarm. If you see the Provost Vonny Stockmann refusing tap water, it's simply because she's not thirsty.'

Vonny   You're being ridiculous.

Kirsten   Drink it then. Drink it and I'll write your statement.

Pause. **Vonny** *picks up the glass.*

Vonny   Fine then.

She chucks its contents back into the sink.

Vonny   We'll do it your way.

Kirsten   Okey dokey.

Vonny   You don't get to push me around, Kirsten. I tried to warn you. Good luck.

Vonny *leaves.*

Kirsten *takes out her phone. She opens WhatsApp, and messages* **Benny**.

The text reads:

Kirsten*: I spoke to my sister. Not good.*

Grey tick. Two grey ticks. A wait. The ticks all turn blue.

Benny*: Ah.*

Kirsten*: Pretty spectacularly not good.*

Benny*: Right.*

Kirsten*: So I guess it looks like we've got a fight on our hands then, eh?*

Benny*: Yas! Fucking come on then! [Flame emoji.]*

Kirsten*: Too right. Fuck her. [Fist bump emoji.]*

Scene Seven

A barrage of social media posts, vox-pops, radio call-ins, responses to **Aly***'s #BigSplashLaunch hashtag. A digital whirlwind of anticipation and excitement. 'Best thing to happen in this Town in generations, no question.' 'New jobs, a brighter future, and hopefully our new visitors can get a different, more positive view of the place.' 'Aly, if I could just say, I started my new job on the resort a few weeks ago and so I've seen all behind the scenes and that, and can I just say it is just absolutely fantastic. . .'*

Aly   Yes folks, great stuff all this. Just a rumour that we might have some major news coming in that is relevant to today's revelries. Can't say any more for now, but some pretty big, big news. Stay tuned so that you're not the last to know –

Vonny*'s car.* **Vonny** *sits in the passenger seat, alone.* **Benny** *arrives, outside. He looks over his shoulder, and enters.* **Vonny** *hands him hand sanitiser. He obliges.*

Benny   This is all a bit fucking clandestine is it no? You got me something juicy? Can I say a 'senior source'?

Vonny   I spoke to my sister.

Benny   Right. Aye? How's she getting on, how's the speech coming on?

Vonny   Don't be an arsehole, Benny.

Benny   What?

Vonny   I know about the story.

Benny   What story?

Vonny   I don't want this to get difficult, Benny, you know that. I really don't. I want you to help me do the right thing here. My sister has the situation completely blown out of proportion –

Benny   Here, listen here I'm a journalist and last I checked we don't talk to politicians about what stories we are or aren't going to run in advance in this country –

Vonny   It's death to this town, Benny. I know you don't want that. Without the resort it –

Benny   Ach, don't give me that, the town'll be fine. Well it'll be shite, but just the same level of shite. You're scared about what this means for you. Well, fair enough. I still think you could make good on this, if you get out on the front foot –

Vonny   I'm not giving you a fucking interview if that's what you mean.

Benny   Suit yourself.

Vonny   You have to kill the story, Benny.

Benny   Because what, you say so?

Vonny   Well I was hoping to appeal to your basic sense of right and wrong first, but okay then. Fine. Because I say so.

Benny   Like she cannae just go ahead and post whatever she wants online anyway, I'm just trying to get in on it –

Vonny   Aye but there are *ways* of putting ideas in their proper *context* and that is something that you can help me with –

Benny   Don't patronise me Vonny, love. I don't know what you think this is with your shady wee meetings in poxy wee car parks like you're in the fucking *Wire*, but see if you think for a minute that Benny Hovstad is such a shitey journalist that he'd suppress information in the clear public interest to further the career of some wee smout of a politician, then you'd better think again, alright? Your wee sister has done an important, brilliant thing here. And she deserves our support.

Vonny Are you finished?

Benny No, actually, I'm not finished. We've got a free press in case you forgot. The most vital function of democracy. This stuff is what people like me live for, this is the stuff that's in our blood. Speaking truth to power. And you, sweetheart, are about to get your first big taste of what it feels like to be in power and have the truth spoken to you. Right in your stupid wee face. So there. Aye. Now I'm done. If this is all you've got here then I am done with you. So take your wee power flex and shove it up your arse. Ya stuck up cow.

Vonny You think I don't know about the intern lassies, Benny?

Beat.

Vonny I mean, if you're done you're done of course but I just thought you might be interested in these emails I happen to have here. Oh. You're staying. Okay good. Well. This one here is from a lassie telling me about how you used to grab her arse every morning. She also has a heartwarming story about being sent to the shops to buy you some johnnies before the staff night out –

Benny Come on. Show me that. When are these from, these are what, fifteen-year-old these stories I bet you. Workplace banter. Old school maybe, not proud of it but that's the way it was. If this is your idea some kind of kompromat then –

Vonny This one talks about 'an archaic and dehumanising culture of male entitlement,' that was from someone who worked with you in 2019. She says it was 'a belittling and degrading environment for unpaid female employees.'

Benny Unpaid! We're broke! Why do you think we relocated back to this shit-hole. Do you have any idea how many journalists we've laid off in the last five years, we cannae pay bloody interns for God's sake!

Vonny Spoken like a true union man, well done. Solidarity forever. It says here she was scared to say anything because you would ruin her career, but left the job with such a damaged sense of self-worth that she never worked again anyway. Look at this.

'He used to come in to work smelling of booze, it was frightening to be around him. On one occasion, with nobody around, he told me to cheer up and give him a kiss, and when I refused he forced his tongue into my throat –'

Benny   Never happened. Dunno who the fuck she is or what she's talking about, lying wee bitch.

Vonny   Steady on big man. These lying wee bitches have also passed me this.

She shows **Benny** *a picture on her phone.*

Benny   I WAS DRUNK. IT WAS SENT IN ERROR, IT WASN'T EVEN ME WHO –

Vonny   That was sent from your email account, to every single member of staff including –

Benny   I was very, very drunk – it was the Christmas party, there was a few of us just arsing about, I made a full apology, we dealt with –

Vonny   – including an intern who had not yet turned seventeen. A schoolgirl, working weekends. Not legally a child. But about as close as it comes.

Silence.

Benny   I don't appreciate being threatened like this, this is not –

Vonny   I don't see it as a threat, Benny. More like a peace offering. See, it'd be nice if we could stay pals wouldn't it? It's good to have friends isn't it? People to look out for you. See your old mucker here has managed to convince these women to stay quiet for now –

Benny   How?

Vonny   Ways and means.

Benny   Ways and means?

Vonny   Ways and fucking means, Benny, aye.

Benny   What ways and means like?

Vonny   I don't need to tell you that, that's my business. You're welcome by the way. Suffice to say it involves a cast-iron guarantee that no women working under you will have to suffer anything like this ever again, which seems fair. But there are also some conditions for me –

Benny   You're bluffing. If anyone is gonna make a noise over any of this nonsense they'd have done it by now, or they'll do it anyway, you don't have any sway over this at all. Nice try.

Vonny   Okay. Okay, fine so let's find out. You go public with your story, and tomorrow I'll go public with mine. Since I don't have any control over the situation anyway, what difference does it make, right? Or, we could go with my suggestion. And see if all of this stays under wraps.

Beat.

Vonny   Ways and means, Benny. Let's stay pals. Okay? Don't run the fucking story.

Scene Eight

Kirsten *and* **Benny***, in a quiet corner of a pub.*

Kirsten   – I think you are going to absolutely love me by the way, because this is really actually quite good. Fuck it, it's *really* good. Listen to this bit: 'That this corruption of our water, our most fundamental life source, looks to have been caused by the council fast-tracking a project that was intended to promote health and wellbeing adds cruel insult to an already deep and violent injury.' Boom! Do you think my sister would have let me write that? No chance. You know what, I'm glad – I am actually glad that she decided to be a dick about it. Imagine we'd had to dance around her the whole time? This way we just get to tell the truth. The simple, uncompromising, honest *truth*. Isn't that the absolute least people deserve? 'The light of truth has been cast over some of the darker corners of this town and it's a light that will now surely only

grow. Who knows where it will lead us?' Ha! Take that Vonny,
ya cow.

Benny   Kirsten.

Kirsten   I know, I know. I know that you and Aly are both
wanting to put me front and centre in this, make me into some kind
of hero of the story and all that –

Benny   Kirst –

Kirsten   – I mean I'm not saying I'm not a hero, maybe I am a
hero. I mean why not?

Benny   We're not –

Kirsten   You'd accept being the hero, if it was your discovery,
wouldn't you? Too right. Aly would. Why should I pretend I'm not
a hero? Well fine. Fine then. If people want to call me a hero why
shouldn't they?

Benny   We're not running it, Kirsten. The story. We're not
running it.

Kirsten   What do you mean?

Benny   I can't explain just now. I will later, I promise. I'm really
sorry for leading you on. But it's a bad idea. The story is a very bad
idea. That's all you need to know. I'm sorry.

Kirsten   No, no, no, no – no. No. No. It's a *good* idea. A *good*
idea Benny remember? Speaking truth to power!

Benny   I'll explain later. I've brought Aly up to speed. I got ahead
of myself, and I apologise.

Kirsten   What's happened?

Benny   On reflection, I suppose, I don't think you have sufficient
proof for such a massive undertaking.

Benny's *phone beeps. He looks. Projected text: 'Vonny: let me
know how you go. If she goes ahead anyway, I have a plan.' His
face sinks.*

Kirsten   What's she done? Come on tell me, what has she said to you?

Benny   Who?

Kirsten   Unbelievable. Right. Right, fine. I'll do it without you then. No bother, Benny. No bother at all.

Benny   Kirsten. I'm speaking as your friend here, and you need to listen to me. Have you thought about your own position, in all of this?

Kirsten   The truth is the thing that matters and we need to get it out fast, that's what *you* said –

Benny   You are in over your head. Okay? That's the clearest warning I can give you. If you keep pursuing this –

Kirsten   There is *literal fucking poison* coming out of your kitchen taps Benny are you mental?

Benny   What I'm saying is that on reflection I don't think you have sufficient proof for such a –

Kirsten   Oh Jesus Christ!

Benny   We're dropping the story, Kirsten, and so should you.

Kirsten *gathers up her stuff.*

Benny   Don't do anything stupid. Kirsten.

Kirsten *leaves.*

Scene Nine

Kirsten, *staring at her laptop screen, which we see projected; an unpublished Medium post entitled 'What Lies Beneath: The Truth About The Big Splash Resort And The Poison In YOUR Water by Kirsten Stockmann'. The cursor hovers over the 'publish' button. She stares, deliberating.*

Vonny *stands behind a camera in front of* **Aly**, *who is hurriedly adjusting himself. She gives him a thumbs up.*

Aly   Hey troops, just logging back on with a brief announcement from the people at the Big Splash resort who've asked us to read this short statement to keep you all in the loop with some developments. Here goes.

'We at Big Splash Holiday Resort are sad and sorry to announce that one of our founding Executive Directors, Kirsten Stockmann, has stepped down from upcoming duties on the grounds of emotional and mental health difficulties. We wish Kirsten all the best in dealing with these personal issues, and ask that you respect her privacy.

The launch of the resort will go ahead as planned tonight in conjunction with the launch of the town's bid for UK City of Regeneration, though Ms Stockmann will of course no longer be in attendance. We're all sure Kirsten would want it to go *swimmingly* and for it to be as wonderful a celebration of this town as possible.'

Well. Not the news I expected to be bringing you there and uh, very sad news. I'm honoured to know Kirsten personally myself having met her recently and I extend my warmest wishes to her, and her family.

Petra *looks at her phone. She is horror-struck.* **Vonny** *switches the camera off.*

Aly   So here what the fu –

Vonny   It's fine. It's all fine, don't worry. You look great.

Kirsten   Fuck em.

Kirsten *hits send. Her piece is published. It's out there. She takes a deep breath.*

Benny *looks at his phone.*

Benny   Ah, bollocks.

Benny *calls* **Vonny**. **Vonny** *picks up.*

Benny   She's done it. She's published the story.

Vonny   Course she has.

Benny She's tagged in all the national news outlets, the council, government, everyone.

Vonny So take control of the situation then.

Vonny *hangs up.*

Benny Ah Christ!

Scene Ten

An overlapping multimedia cacophony of voices. Audio snatches from radio phone-ins: 'I mean she's mental. I know you cannae say that anymore but that's what they've said. If she's saying this mad stuff then that's a shame for her like, but that's all it is –' 'Look, the thing is, if there's any doubt about it all we need to get it checked out don't we? What are the council doing? Are we getting bottled water delivered? Are we nothing!' 'I went to school with her and there was always something wrong with her, she had this, this evil energy about her . . .' 'She practically got given the job by her sister it's gross nepotism . . .' etc. Fragments of news footage; **Aly** *singing to adoring fans at an open mic night as a regional news reporter narrates recent developments. Shaky camera-phone footage posted online; some schoolkids harassing* **Petra** *for her mum being mental, chucking water at her, she throws out a hand and wipes the screen. Concerned messages in a school parents WhatsApp group: 'He's not been able to eat for days. They don't know what's wrong. He's screaming saying he feels like he's burning inside.' 'They've taken her into hospital, she's being fed on a drip. They said she's lucky to be there, they're running out of beds. . .' Scrolling projections of social media posts and below-the-line article comments: 'Here what if she has a point? Will you be having a shower tonight? I won't! This needs investigated!' 'I don't see anything wrong with the water. Tired of being patronised by so-called experts.' 'Why can't we just have nice things in this town without some London wanker turning it into a story about us all drinking piss or whatever. I hate this.' etc.*

In the middle of all this is **Kirsten**. *She tries to reply, perhaps, to every tweet, every post, but it's all too much. She tries to switch off* *from it. Closing her laptop, switching off her phone, but more and more screens keep flickering on around her as the noise intensifies.*

Scene Eleven

Petra, *with* **Derek**. **Derek** *has an arm around her. She has been crying.* **Kirsten** *arrives.*

Kirsten   Petra, for God's sake – I've been looking everywhere. Will you not answer your bloody phone? Petra? Petra, get in the car. There's something we need to talk about.

Derek   She's heard. Are you okay, love?

Kirsten   Don't call me that. Petra. It's okay. It'll be okay. She can't actually just force me out of a job, I mean – look I just need you to get into the car please.

Derek   Do as your mother says, Petra.

Kirsten   Keep out of this will you.

Petra   Everyone at school says you're mental.

Kirsten   Don't listen to them, it's just daft nonsense. It's your auntie being a – she's trying to undermine me. That's all. And it won't work. Because I'm right. So don't worry about that. Okay?

Petra   Someone called you a junkie.

Kirsten   What?

Petra   And someone else said you're a terrorist.

Kirsten   What? That's just kids being ridiculous love, that's just bullies making up nonsense. You have to credit their imaginations, I dunno what they'll come up with next –

Derek   Have you not read the article?

Kirsten   What article?

Petra *reads from her phone.*

Petra   'The Tragic Story of Provost Stockmann's Wayward Sister. After the surprise resignation of Kirsten Stockmann from the blah blah blah we look into the troubled past of this tragic figure and the unfortunate mistakes that led to her appointment.'

Kirsten   What the fuck.

Petra   'Her profound mental health difficulties.'

Kirsten   What?

Petra   'The drug-fuelled parties of her youth.'

Kirsten   I mean that's just parties, that's just student parties –

Petra   'Her criminal record and unlawful activities in London with known domestic extremists.'

Kirsten   I was a member of Greenpeace. It was a protest.

Petra   'Her promiscuous past and teenage pregnancy to tragic son of local businessman.'

Kirsten   Fucking hell, Petra, I'm sorry –

Petra   Why are they doing this to us?

Kirsten   Who on Earth is publishing this nonsense?

Derek   Your pal.

Petra   Creepy McCreepface.

Kirsten   No, come on.

Derek   Fraid so. Benny Hovstad has written a hit piece on you Kirsten. Dunno what your sister's got on him but it must be bloody good.

Kirsten   Petra, get in the car.

Derek   I just want to say –

Kirsten   Get in the car, Petra.

Derek   If I can just say – it's good what you're doing. Brave. It takes chutzpah. So – you just keep at them. Okay? Just so you stick it to them.

Kirsten   I thought you said it was all moonshine. Cockroaches. A big laugh.

Derek   I believe you, Kirsten. And, if the truth's on your side then people will see that soon enough. So keep it up.

Kirsten   Why are you saying this?

Derek   Just trying to do my bit for, like, sticking up for the family. That's all. And also, because, you know. I'm proud of you – of your courage.

Kirsten   Okay. Well thank you.

Derek   In your piece you said it was – connected. To my, uh, my land. Is that right? It's coming from my land? From the dump?

Kirsten   Fraid so.

Derek   Right.

Kirsten   Petra, let's go.

Derek   Well we'll see to that.

Kirsten   Petra, we're going.

Derek   Right. Okay. Right. We'll see to that.

Scene Twelve

A continuing cascade of social media posts and news clips. A Buzzfeed-style reporter hounds a nervous **Aly** *down the street. Online threats and abuse directed at* **Kirsten***, increasingly misogynistic and hateful in tone. Some of it targets* **Petra***, some of it threatens to dox them by posting their address. Other conflicted voices of doubt, and fear. The online story escalating to national news. Either onstage or onscreen we see* **Kirsten** *opening a door, being met with a mob of paparazzi, slamming the door shut again. Everything arrives in a hurry, fragmented, bombarding. In and through this,* **Aly***, onstage, picks up a phone and calls someone.* **Benny** *answers.*

Benny   What?

Aly   I thought you said the water thing was a mistake? What's actually happening here?

Benny   The woman is deluded, okay, like I said. An error of judgement on my part –

Aly   It's all getting a bit out of hand is it no?

Benny   You know how much people want this thing to go ahead right?

Aly   Well aye, what do you think I've been doing all day? Some of the abuse she's getting is fucking brutal, like genuinely –

Benny   A bit spicy maybe. That's the internet for you –

Aly   I dunno –

Benny   Listen. You're an influential man Aly. You're well-loved around here, you know that. And if you want to start telling folk that you think Kirsten Stockmann has a point that's your prerogative alright? But see all that shite they're saying about her? You have to ask yourself whether you want that to be you. That's all.

Aly   What are you saying like?

Benny   We've all seen how easily the switch of public opinion can flip. And if you're not careful, it will eat you alive. Just think carefully mate, that's all I'm saying.

Aly   Look. Just tell me. Is the water safe or not?

Benny   Aye. The water's safe. As far as we know.

Aly   Right. Right, well that's fine then. That's fine.

Benny   See you in a couple of hours then. We're all looking forward to your DJ set!

The media onslaught continues. All the while **Kirsten***, physically forcing her way through it all onstage, exhausted, until –*

Scene Thirteen

Kirsten *and* **Petra** *'s house.* **Kirsten** *stares, stunned, a shell of a person. Silence.*

Petra   Right. Gimme your phone.

Kirsten   What?

Petra   Phone. Give it here.

Kirsten   What for like?

Petra   The guy from the campaign. Twitch guy. Popstar.

Kirsten   Aly? Ach, I wouldn't –

Petra   It's ringing.

Aly *watches his phone ring. Considers answering. Doesn't.* **Petra** *rings again.* **Aly** *picks up the phone this time, rejects the call.* **Petra** *puts the phone down.*

Kirsten   He's hung up hasn't he? He's hung up.

Petra   Voicemail. Wanker!

Kirsten *'s phone beeps.* **Petra** *looks at it.*

Petra   Why the fuck are you still getting Twitter notifications on this?

Kirsten   I don't know how to switch them off.

Petra   Right. I'm deleting your account.

Kirsten   What is it?

Petra   Nothing just –

Kirsten   What is it, Petra?

Petra   More of the same. Death threats. Rape threats. All the bantz.

Kirsten   I didn't want you to have to see that, love –

Petra   Well, I don't want you to have to see it either, so – blip blap bloop. Deleted. Done.

Kirsten   I'm sorry.

Kirsten *starts to cry.*

Kirsten   I'm sorry. I've ruined it. I've ruined everything.

Petra   Mum. It's okay – you haven't! Please don't –

Kirsten   This was supposed to be it, Petra, our big chance. I was trying to set us up in a place where we could be stable, secure.

Petra   Mum.

Kirsten   I'm sorry.

Silence.

Kirsten   We're really fucked now, Petra.

Pause.

Kirsten   My God what am I gonna do for money?

Pause.

Kirsten   I should just call Vonny now, tell her I'll write her statement and maybe –

Petra   Mum, stop it.

Kirsten   They are targeting *you* now, Petra. I have to make this stop. I'll call Vonny and tell her I'll settle –

Petra   No! Mum! Fuck that. No. Did Chief Brody settle? Did he go 'okay then fine I'll just drop this'? When the Mayor refused to listen to him and refused to close the beaches even though they all knew there was a fucking shark out there, did Brody just shrug and go 'alright then, I suppose let's just *settle*'? Did he bollocks! He found a crazy old pirate and a fish scientist and went out to sea to catch that fucking shark like some kind of unstoppable Captain Ahab Moby Dick legend!

Kirsten   What the hell are you on about, Petra?

Petra *Jaws*. We watched it in Ms Quinn's Media Studies class. Only saw the first forty-five minutes, I'm guessing he catches the shark in the end right?

Kirsten Yes. Yes he does.

Petra See I knew it! I bet he swims out and kills that bastard shark with his own two hands!

Kirsten That's actually exactly what he does, aye.

Petra Well. There you go then. Do that.

Kirsten I don't think I can sweetheart. I don't think I have it in me anymore.

Petra Fine. I'll do it then.

Petra *leaves.* **Kirsten** *follows her.*

Kirsten Petra. Petra!

Scene Fourteen

*The space is transformed and we are in THE BIG SPLASH
RESORT for the digital launch event.* **Aly** *performs a beatbox and
DJ set. It is sick! With him, co-hosting the launch event, is* **Vonny**,
with **Benny** *also present. A boisterous live audience of townsfolk is
joined by a much larger audience tuning in online. Their responses
to events are visible throughout in the form of live text chat like on
Twitch, Youtube, and Facebook Live broadcasts.*

Aly Whoop whoop! Thank you! Thanks very much, you're all fantastic. More tunes coming up but first we've got a few speakers here to say a few words as we launch the good ship Big Splash on its maiden voyage. As most of you – all of you, probably uh, probably know, we've had to make a few last-minute changes to our line-up so – uh, consequently our first speaker this evening is the leader of our council the, woman who grabbed this whole project by the uh, the knackers and dragged it over the finish line, the formidable, the indomitable Vonny Stockman. Come on up here Vonny!

Enthusiasm in the chat for **Vonny***! Emoji applause!*

Vonny   Thank you. Thanks very much.

She looks at her notes.

Vonny   Determination. Grit. Strength. Pride. These are the words I think of when I think about our town. And yet, when others speak about us, they often talk of these things as if in the past tense. 'A once-proud town' is a phrase we're all surely far too familiar with.

Vonny   The truth is we have always been proud of our community. But now – at last – we have something to show for it. A top-class facility, for top-class folk. Ensuring our people, our men, our women, our children can grow healthy, happy, and full of *life*. This is our brand new Big Splash –

Petra *bursts into the room, followed by* **Kirsten***.*

Petra   Let Kirsten Stockmann speak!

Silence.

Petra   My mum is here and she'd like to say a few words –

Vonny   They are not supposed to be here!

Benny   Pull the broadcast, Aly, for fucksake!

Petra   Don't you fucking dare!

Aly *stands frozen. The broadcast runs on. Big WTF energy in the chat!*

Aly   Everyone, we have a – we have a bit of a strange one. There is a guest who –

Vonny   Aw Jesus.

Aly   Kirsten Stockmann, for you all watching at home, Kirsten was originally a scheduled speaker, and there has been a request to –

Vonny   Get them out of here! Get her out! This is ridiculous!

Petra   You're ridiculous!

Benny   She's not allowed here!

Aly   Can everyone. Just. Shut. The fuck! Up! For a minute!

Silence.

Aly   I think we should hear her out.

Vonny   You fucking wally.

Aly *mutes/unplugs* **Vonny**'s *mic*

Vonny   This is outrageous!

Outrage in the chat! 'I heard she's a terrorist!' 'She's not a terrorist ya fanny!' 'Aye let her speak!' 'Chuck her out!' etc.

Aly   Kirsten will you come up here please.

Benny   Fucking hell.

Kirsten *approaches the stage/broadcast area. The chat goes wild!*

Kirsten, *shattered, rinsed, absolutely through the wringer, steps up to the mic. Silence. She stands, stoic and resolved. She appears to look every member of the crowd and audience in the eye.*

Kirsten   Hello. Contrary to what you might have been told, or what you might have read or heard, I'm not deluded. All I've tried to do from the start of this is to present you with the evidence. The reality of how things are. I've taken the position that that's the most respectful thing a person can do, simply presenting the truth, however difficult or inconvenient or even nightmarish. The honest truth.

And the truth is there is another sickness running through this town, maybe even worse, even more harmful, than the poison in our water. The horrible, sickening abuse my daughter and I have been subject to today is repulsive enough on its own, but it's only one symptom of an utterly sick society. A society that presents itself as a fair and liberal democracy but in truth is built on nothing other than outright lies, manipulation, and bullying. All at the hands of our self-serving politicians, corrupt, destructive businesses, and spineless, grovelling press.

Benny   Aly, get her mic out for God's sake!

Vonny   She can't just –

Aly   Everyone will you just shut it!

*As **Kirsten** speaks, the comments in the chat respond, increasingly fast, and wild.*

Kirsten   But you don't need me to tell you this. You know it already, you're not idiots. We all know it don't we? Every one of you, everybody here, everybody listening to this, knows about this sickness. And yet it's almost as if we've come to accept it as some sort of tolerable or even normal feature of who we are. A cancer that we've decided to just live with, and somehow try to ignore. Like an ant that is eaten alive from the inside out by some kind of parasite. We go about our lives, wearing this outside appearance of a normal functioning democracy. Pretending. When the truth is, on the inside, the body of it all is diseased and rotten and putrid to the core. And we all know it.

Let me just say before I go on, that I really do have enormous affection for this place, my home town. I was young when I left and although my sister will tell you not to see me as one of your own, I am. The years I spent away from here always felt like a kind of exile if I'm totally honest. And it broke my heart. In the years away, I developed a kind of rose-tinted nostalgia for this place, for its people. Well, today has truly put paid to that.

See what I've discovered is that it's not the politicians, the press, or the money men who are your real enemies here. No. It's *you*. It's *yourselves*. The people of this town.

Aly   Aw come on you cannae be saying that –

Kirsten   This is the real discovery I've made today. You the people. Complacently, idly believing whatever lie is told to you as long as it makes you feel rewarded, and good about yourselves, and comfortable. Day after day, decade after decade, lining up to just let yourself be shafted from one generation to the next. These people standing before you tonight were ready to let you die.

Vonny   Lies! Misinformation!

Kirsten   And for what? Short-term economic interests and their
own public image. And you were going to let them. Because who
actually wants to rework an entire infrastructure, an entire plumbing
system anyway? Sounds like a lot of hassle and expense am I right?
And for what? Better water? Better lives? A town we can actually
continue to live in? What's wrong with the water we've got already,
haven't they just told us just now that it's fine? In fact we've heard
it's good, we've heard it can't be made any better. Toxic you say?
Pour us another glass and we'll drink it right here. I'm parched
actually, give us another. Fill a bloody pool up and we'll swim in
the stuff. And here, aren't we lucky to even have a pool in the first
place? We were promised a pool. And we like the promise! The
promise is shiny and nice and best of all the promise doesn't
actually ask that we do anything or change anything! Why rock
the boat, right? Why risk trying to change things? Why make a
fuss? Why not just keep your head down and *choose* to just leave
it, and keep things as they are. All the while imagining that it
was never your responsibility in the first place. And so when
things get worse – and they will get worse – and when something
needs to be done, and the sickness simply cannot be ignored any
longer, you can tell yourselves all this is someone else's fault
anyway. How were you to know? You liked the promises you
were made. You just believed what they told you at the time.
You were only going along with what was said. And anyone
who gets in the way, anyone who does something so inconvenient
as to point out the sickness that is killing us, anyone who actually
tries to do something about it, can simply get fucked! Destroy her!
Tear her down, and leave her lying in the mud, the traitor! The
witch! Crush her so completely she'll never want to speak again!
Well fuck you!

You – we – the people of this town have been brutally exploited
and abused and cast aside for generations by a system that hates
us and has always hated us. You don't need me to tell you that.
But Jesus Christ do you have to make it so fucking easy for
them?

And that is the discovery I've made today. You, the people. You cowards. You dickheads. You absolute shitebags. You're your own worst enemy. And you always fucking have been.

Silence and stillness in the chat. Feedback from **Kirsten***'s microphone. And then, absolute fury!*

Vonny   There you have it! Kirsten Stockmann! An enemy of the people!

Aly   Everyone just settle, okay, just settle down! We will not have threats in the chat, we will not –

Vonny   The people watching at home deserve to be heard, in their fullest! If they want to criticise and complain about what they've just seen then by God they have every right –

Kirsten *pushes her way past* **Vonny***, making for the exit.* **Vonny** *pushes her back. They fight! Viciously, like little girls, like quarreling sisters.* **Petra** *grabs* **Kirsten** *and pulls her away.*

Benny   I warned you, I tried to warn you, Kirsten –

Petra   Shut your fucking hole you pervy cunt.

Vonny*, bloody-nosed, reclaims the mic in the broadcast area.*

Vonny   Now we've all heard what she has to say! We can discount it, we can discount her and get back to – everyone – everyone quieten down! Please –

The chat is now just unhinged, on its own trajectory, outrage and fury. 'I know where she fucking lives' etc.

Vonny   Everyone! Everyone watching at home, everyone in the, in the chat – you are right to be angry! I am on your side, you are right to be angry but if you could please – we are going to press on. We are pressing ahead with – everyone! Please –

A deafening crash of NOISE as the ONLINE ANGER spilling out of the event becomes a cavalcade of VIOLENT MOB OUTRAGE. It is DIGITAL CARNAGE!

Scene Fifteen

Rubble, debris, broken glass. **Petra** *enters. She pours herself a bowl of cereal, and sits eating it, as she did the day before at the start of the play.*

Kirsten *enters, still in her clothes from the previous day, bin bag in hand. She surveys the scene in silence. She sets about picking up the mess, as* **Petra** *scrolls her phone. This continues for some time.* **Kirsten** *picks up a small rock. She holds it out to show* **Petra**.

Kirsten   Found another one.

Petra   Be finding a few more yet, I'd have thought.

Beat.

Petra   You know you've torn a big hole in the arse of your trousers as well, yeah?

Kirsten   Ah, shite! Twats.

Petra   You should never go out fighting for truth and justice in your best trousers, mum. Schoolgirl error.

Kirsten   Lesson learned.

Petra *starts playing a video on her phone. We can hear the audio from it. It is footage from last night, filmed on a phone camera.*

Kirsten   . . . You just believed what they told you at the time. You were only going along with what was said. When in fact, in the end, you've only got yourselves to blame for the absolute state of all of this, sickening sorry mess. That's the discovery I've made today. That you are your own worst enemy. You, the people. You cowards. You morons. You absolute shitebags. It's your fault, this mess. And it always fucking has been.

Kirsten   What are you doing?

Petra   Video. From last night. Someone's posted a clip. 'Mad Scientist Kirsten Stockmann makes discovery that we're all a massive pile of arseholes, basically.' Two hundred and eighty-six thousand views so far, apparently.

Kirsten   That's a lot.

Petra   Yeah, you're famous I guess. Yay. Listen to this: 'It is the opinion of this publication that Provost Vonny Stockmann deserves respect and praise for her resolve and determination in the face of the inevitable criticisms that will emerge, whatever comes to light in this impending review. The Provost has repeatedly insisted that the claims made by her sister lack veracity, but has nevertheless agreed to conduct an investigation. That alone should reassure everyone concerned that –'

Kirsten   Is this Benny?

Petra   Yup. Your bestie.

Kirsten   Fuck off.

Petra   Aaaand they've got an interview with Aunty Vonny, check it out.

Vonny   Of course we condemn in no uncertain terms the violence of last night, but we must also acknowledge the strength of feeling there is against those who would try to block the progress of this town.

Kirsten   Strength of feeling, Vonny? They smashed my fucking windows in.

Vonny   That strength of feeling is real, it is apparent all over social media, it's apparent in the streets, and we should listen to it. Yes, the opening of the Big Splash Resort will now be delayed – this is principally for minor repairs, and the accompanying review will undoubtedly put to rest any –

Petra *switches it off.*

Kirsten   Cow.

Petra   Still though. A review eh? That's something.

Kirsten *starts packing various things into cardboard boxes.* **Petra** *watches.*

Petra   Where we gonna go?

Kirsten   I dunno.

Petra   I mean, I don't think you're really gonna get much work round here now that you're the internet lady calling the people of the town every cunt under the sun.

Kirsten   Petra.

Petra   Just saying.

Beat.

Kirsten   London. We'll go back to London again, I don't know. You can see your old pals again. That'll be nice.

Beat.

Petra   You weren't happy there. Were you?

Kirsten   No. No I wasn't.

Beat.

Kirsten   Australia then. This whole blasted rainy island can do one. Berlin. Somewhere European. That'd be nice.

Petra   How we gonna afford that?

Kirsten   Dunno. We're not.

Petra   And wouldn't you need a visa?

Kirsten   I haven't thought it through alright. I'm not good at this.

Beat.

Kirsten   I don't know what we'll do, Petra. I'm sorry. But I don't.

They clean up together, **Kirsten** *unable to look at* **Petra**.

A knock on the door. They look at each other.

Kirsten   I'll go.

Kirsten *exits, leaving* **Petra** *momentarily alone and nervous. She re-enters with* **Derek Kilmartin**.

Petra   Grandad!

Derek   Hello sweetheart.

Derek *gives* **Petra** *a kiss on the head.*

Derek   Jings. A fine mess, this place. Still. Plenty of fresh air in through these windows, I'd have thought. So, every cloud.

Kirsten   Is there something in particular I can help you with or have you just come to take the piss?

Petra   Mum.

Derek   It's alright, it's alright. It's been a stressful time, for everyone. Here. Let me put the kettle on.

Derek *goes to the kettle. He goes to fill it up from the sink, then stops. He fills it up with bottled water, then flicks it on.*

Derek   Who wants tea? A good cup of tea will help yous feel better. And besides, I'm here with what I hope will be a bit of welcome good news.

Derek *plants a briefcase on the table.*

Derek   Anyone want to guess what's in this?

Petra   It's not another massive ice cream, is it?

Derek   Much better than that.

Derek *opens the briefcase, takes out a laptop, opens it on a screen displaying company shares.*

Petra   What's this?

Derek   These, Petra, are shares.

Kirsten   Shares?

Derek   Good old-fashioned shares. In the baths.

Kirsten   In the resort you mean?

Derek   They were not very difficult to get hold of today, I can tell you.

Kirsten   And you've bought –

Derek   As many as I could possibly pay for, aye. In fact, you are both standing in the company of the new *majority shareholder*. Which sort of makes me the boss of the place.

Petra   Ha ha, what the fuck.

Kirsten   What on Earth have you gone and done that for? You're aware of the state of the place's reputation, those shares are utterly worthless –

Derek   Well, they were certainly available on the cheap aye, let's say that much. Folk couldn't get out of there quick enough.

Kirsten   So what are you playing at? I don't get it.

Derek   The reputation of the place, Kirsten, is something you'll be able to help me turn around. If you're a good girl.

Kirsten   A good girl.

Petra   Grandad, ew.

Derek   You'd said in the wee piece that you put on the internet that the source of this – pollution shall we call it – was related to the, eh, the business activities taking place on my land, is that right?

Kirsten   That's right. And you said you'd sort it.

Derek   Exactly. And that's what we'll do. See, I couldn't sit silent on something like that, could I? I know I'm not a well-liked man around here, Kirsten. But I've always put that down to jealousy, as opposed to any actual harm I might have caused anyone. I've always taken good care of my image. These allegations – they're not great for me. It's dirty. It's a bad dirty look, and at the end of the day it's bad for business. I've lived in this town my whole life. I've built what I have from nothing. And I intend to go out a clean man, Kirsten, with a clean reputation.

Kirsten   Well I'm afraid you've shat the bed a bit with that one Derek –

Derek   I don't think so. See that's where you come in. Like a holiday visit to a state-of-the-art spa resort, you are going to *cleanse* me, Kirsten.

Kirsten   Is that right aye.

Derek   The shares as I said, were easy enough to get hold off. But it's still tricky to pull together the capital in such a short time you know. It's all tied up in this, that, or the other. So do you know what money I bought these shares with? No, of course you don't. There was this wee side fund I had for money that was gonna go to Petra after I'm gone –

Petra   Grandad, what?

Derek   Ach, your mum wanted me to tell you about it, what with the way things have been. And I don't think you knew quite how much was in there did you, Kirsten? Or *was* in there, rather. Now it's here. Wrapped up in these, as you say, utterly worthless shares.

Petra   Grandad what the fuck?

Derek   Don't worry sweetheart, I promised you both didn't I, that I would support you. And I will. All you have to do is retract this moonshine you've been putting out about my land.

Derek *takes a bunch of papers out of the briefcase.*

Derek   My lawyers have it all written up but you can add some of your own creative flair, within reason. Of course there is also some paperwork to make sure you don't go off the rails again – I don't like to use the phrase 'gagging order' but you get the gist. We shake hands, our reputations are slowly restored. We let this business with your sister and the water run its course, you get your job back in time, when things have died down. And we run a successful wee family venture together in relative comfort. Or the alternative is, the opposite. The absolute opposite of that for you both, on every count.

The kettle clicks off.

Derek   Who wanted tea? I won't bother if it's just myself. Come on, let's have a cup of tea to celebrate.

Petra   Grandad, I can't fucking believe you!

Derek   Aye, kids can be fiery about these things. And you were fiery too when you were Petra's age, Kirsten! But it's fair to say that's got you into a bit of bother over the years hasn't it? And as grown adults – no disrespect now, Petra – we understand how the world works. We know what principles *really* are. And what greater principle is there, than looking after the long-term wellbeing of your own family, your own daughter? You'd be crazy, absolutely barking mad, not to. So now we get to find out if you actually are a principled woman, Kirsten. Or if you really are just a fucking heidcase after all.

Petra   Mum, say something, tell him.

Derek   No, no, Don't worry. Take some time to think it over. It always feels better that way. I'll call in on you again later. Here, I'll leave this pen though, just in case you can't find one. Tattie bye.

Derek *exits.*

Petra   Mum.

Beat.

Petra   Mum, you're not actually thinking of –

Kirsten   I don't know what I should do, Petra, I don't –

Petra   If you say yes to that I will never look at you in the same way again.

Beat.

Petra   And not like, in a good way. I mean like in a bad way, obviously. The bad one of that.

Beat.

Petra   You can't agree to this, Mum. I won't let you.

Kirsten   Just – just keep packing up for now, and –

Petra   Mum.

Kirsten   Aye?

Petra   I don't actually really want to keep moving all the time.

Kirsten   Okay. So I sign the paper and we do what he says –

Petra   No, I mean. I don't want to move. But I don't want to do that either.

Kirsten   You can't mean staying here like this love, surely?

Petra *shrugs.*

Petra   I don't think we should let them push us around. I don't think we should have to go because they don't like us. And I don't think you should have to lie for us to stay. You said this place is my home. Our home. And maybe it is. That's what I think. I think we should stay. And fuck 'em.

Petra   Stay, and be right. And keep saying what's right. And keep staying. And rinse and repeat and, well, we'll be proved right eventually. Probably. Maybe. And then they'll all just have to catch up. And then they'll be sorry. And even if they're not – well –

Kirsten   I don't know, Petra.

Petra   We've already won, really. They just don't know it yet.

Kirsten   It's difficult, Petra. It's difficult being so alone –

Petra   We'll be alright. We've got each other.

Pause. **Petra** *hands her the legal paperwork.*

Petra   Here. Tear it. Tear it up.

Kirsten   Oh, Petra I don't know –

Petra   Yes you do. You do. Tear it.

Kirsten *takes the paper. Thinks. Then rips it.*

Petra   Yes!

Petra *grabs some paper and tears it too. They scrunch it up and tear it into confetti and throw it around and stamp on it, laughing.*

Petra   Shove it up your arse! Shove it up your arse!

Kirsten   Fucking hell, Petra. Oh God –

The paperwork thoroughly pulverised, they stop.

Petra   Well that's that answered then.

Kirsten   Petra?

Petra   Mm?

Kirsten   You really are a wee terror you know that? You're a total riot.

Petra   Yeah. I got that from someone I think. Gimme a bag. Let's just keep cleaning up.

They clean up the mess together, picking up pieces of rubble and of torn paper and depositing each in bin bags. It takes a long time. As they work together, the shared giddy excitement fades. An uncertainty falls on **Kirsten** *as she watches her daughter, full of rebellious optimism, preparing for a future that will undoubtedly hurt her. Has she done the right thing? Will she change her mind? As they continue tidying, they are together, but very apart, as the reality of their uncertain future unfolds in the mess of this life. They continue cleaning, in silence, as the lights fade out.*

End of play.